AngularJS Testing Cookbook

Eliminate volatile code by taking control and understanding how to test AngularJS applications

Simon Bailey

BIRMINGHAM - MUMBAI

AngularJS Testing Cookbook

First published: March 2015

Production reference: 1240315

Published by Packt Publishing Ltd.
Livery Place
35 Livery Street
Birmingham B3 2PB, UK.

ISBN 978-1-78398-374-2

www.packtpub.com

Credits

Author

Simon Bailey

Reviewers

Ashutosh Das

Abhishek Dey

James Morgan

Steve Perkins

Commissioning Editor

Pramila Balan

Acquisition Editor

Richard Brookes-Bland

Content Development Editor

Anand Singh

Technical Editor

Rohith Rajan

Copy Editor

Pranjali Chury

Project Coordinator

Akash Poojary

Proofreaders

Simran Bhogal

Maria Gould

Paul Hindle

Indexer

Tejal Soni

Production Coordinator

Conidon Miranda

Cover Work

Conidon Miranda

About the Author

Simon Bailey is a frontend developer based in the UK, specializing in JavaScript development and application architecture. He founded Newtriks Ltd. and has been remotely contracting for the last 10 years for global corporations and venture-backed start-ups. He regularly consults Angular, Backbone, and React, and trains programmers in test-driven development. He is an enthusiastic open source contributor and maintains a blog at `http://newtriks.com` and is the cofounder and lead developer of the live webcasting platform Sayansho Ltd. He is a husband, father, and lover of the golden age of hip hop.

Gratitude and love goes to my wife Donna, and children Iola, Joel, and Clarisse, for their support and encouragement. Thanks to my parents for their support and persistent pushes in the right direction. Thanks to the amazing network of developers offering help and support to the community.

About the Reviewers

Abhishek Dey, born in West Bengal, India, is a graduate student at the University of Florida, Gainesville, conducting research in the fields of computer security, computer networks, compiler design, analysis of algorithms, and concurrency and parallelism. He is a passionate programmer who started programming in C and Java at the age of 10 and developed a strong interest in web technologies when he was 15. He possesses profound expertise in developing high-volume software using C#, C++, Java, JavaScript, jQuery, AngularJS, and HTML5.

He is a Microsoft Certified Professional, an Oracle Certified Java Programmer, an Oracle Certified Web Component Developer, and an Oracle Certified Business Component Developer.

He has also contributed to bringing about new innovations in the field of Highway Capacity Software Development at McTrans Center at the University of Florida (http://mctrans. ce.ufl.edu/mct/) in collaboration with the Engineering School of Sustainable Infrastructure and Environment (http://www.essie.ufl.edu/).

He has previously reviewed *Kali Linux CTF Blueprints* and *AngularJS UI Development*, both by Packt Publishing.

In his leisure time, Abhishek loves to listen to music, travel to different interesting places, or paint on a canvas giving colors to his imagination. More information about Abhishek Dey can be found at http://abhishekdey.com.

> I'd like to take this opportunity to thank my mom and dad. They are the biggest inspiration of my life.

James Morgan has been working with Angular since early 2011 and immediately fell in love with the programming model drastically different than the traditional request-response model he was used to, and he still continues to promote the use of AngularJS which is necessary for his clients.

AngularJS revolutionized his thinking and approach to the enterprise application stack, and he believes that its widely growing popularity has changed the face of client-side development within the enterprise space forever. A Java and Spring programmer originally, he now spends most of the day working with AngularJS, Node, and Scala. He believes that the up and coming ES6 changes as well as the functional movement within the industry will all compliment AngularJS, and it will continue as a strong first choice for many enterprise applications.

He started his journey with AngularJS inside a small but rapidly growing financial services company based in Manchester, UK, where AngularJS proved its worth as a platform that can live alongside a rapidly changing business and yet comes with the required enterprise features such as dependency injection and testability.

Some of his recent work has been in partnership with Cake Solutions Ltd., a Manchester-based functional software house. He has been an integral member of the team delivering solutions for one of UK's largest price comparison sites as well as for a London-based TV broadcasting company on several internal and client-facing applications. He continues to mentor newcomers to AngularJS and also continues his own professional development and keeps track of the latest changes in Angular and the functional programming world.

I would like to thank my partner for her support over the last few years of late night programming and reading sessions, which may have occasionally hampered her plans.

Steve Perkins is the author of *Hibernate Search by Example* published by Packt Publishing, and has over 15 years of experience working with enterprise Java. He lives in Atlanta, GA, USA, with his wife, Amanda, and their son, Andrew. Steve currently works as an architect at BetterCloud, where he writes software for the Google cloud platform.

When he is not writing code, Steve plays fiddle and guitar and enjoys working with music production software. You can visit his technical blog at `steveperkins.net` and follow him on Twitter at `@stevedperkins`.

www.PacktPub.com

Support files, eBooks, discount offers, and more

For support files and downloads related to your book, please visit www.PacktPub.com.

Did you know that Packt offers eBook versions of every book published, with PDF and ePub files available? You can upgrade to the eBook version at www.PacktPub.com and as a print book customer, you are entitled to a discount on the eBook copy. Get in touch with us at service@packtpub.com for more details.

At www.PacktPub.com, you can also read a collection of free technical articles, sign up for a range of free newsletters and receive exclusive discounts and offers on Packt books and eBooks.

https://www2.packtpub.com/books/subscription/packtlib

Do you need instant solutions to your IT questions? PacktLib is Packt's online digital book library. Here, you can search, access, and read Packt's entire library of books.

Why Subscribe?

- ▶ Fully searchable across every book published by Packt
- ▶ Copy and paste, print, and bookmark content
- ▶ On demand and accessible via a web browser

Free Access for Packt account holders

If you have an account with Packt at www.PacktPub.com, you can use this to access PacktLib today and view 9 entirely free books. Simply use your login credentials for immediate access.

Table of Contents

Preface

It's 2015 and the world has accelerated at a whirlwind pace towards the open source paradigm. Software is now also analyzed and gauged based on GitHub stars, codebase contributors and consistency in Git commits. When Google open sourced AngularJS, it offered a declarative approach for web application development and was welcomed by an ever-growing community. It's been over 4 years since the first commit to the AngularJS codebase and it has evolved at a breakneck speed to become one of the most popular web application frameworks in the world of open-source.

As the AngularJS team cultivated the framework's documentation, it became abundantly clear that they wanted to facilitate testing of web applications. The documented guidance offers solutions on how developers should test but avoids an overly prescriptive testing process. This allows the developer to decide when and where to test, offering a more approachable development workflow, reducing potential concerns surrounding testing.

This book follows the AngularJS philosophy and offers guidance on how to approach testing components that make up the AngularJS framework. Testing need not be a chore. The recipes contained within this book will provide simple accessible solutions to testing, with a clear demarcation of AngularJS-specific functionality between chapters. The benefit of a cookbook is that it can be used as a point of reference for continuous development of your AngularJS applications. Regardless of whether you're starting a project from scratch or looking to introduce tests into an existing codebase, this book will provide you with a reference point to build the testing foundation.

What this book covers

Chapter 1, Setup and Configuration, is crucial in order to get started with the rest of the book and will detail various options for alternative tools that can be used to test AngularJS applications.

Chapter 2, Getting Started with Testing and AngularJS, will form the basis for all tests throughout the book, explaining basics principles required to use Jasmine and AngularJS plus the anatomy of a unit test. Specifics detailed here are crucial to get a test running, for example, dependency injection.

Chapter 3, How to Test Navigation and Routing, will explain how to test routing and page rendering, starting from the view perspective of the application. This chapter also shows how to use Protractor and Page Objects.

Chapter 4, Testing Controllers, explains that the business logic is contained within the controllers, hence it should be addressed early in this book and is the logical early step following routing. Data binding and updating the view based on model data will be tackled ensuring that the UI behaves as expected.

Chapter 5, Testing User Interaction and Directives, focuses on testing changes within a directive based on interaction from either UI events or application updates to the model. Directives are one of the cornerstones of AngularJS and can range in complexity. They can provide the foundation to many aspects of the application and therefore require comprehensive tests.

Chapter 6, Using Spies to Test Events, shows that an application's state can be updated via events, whether from user interaction in the browser or via API changes. We need to ensure that the correct events are sent and with the correct data. We will also test a third party component wrapped in a directive and mimic its events.

Chapter 7, Testing Filters, explains that manipulated output are easily integrated with bound values in the view. They are important to test as they essentially display the data to the user. After looking at a couple of simple examples, this chapter will provide examples on how to run end-to-end tests on filters simulating updates based on events or simulated input.

Chapter 8, Service and Factory Testing with Mocks and Spies, will show recipes on how to use this module to test common HTTP requests. Services form a communication channel with outside services requesting data and feeding it into the application. They are singleton objects and relatively easy to test due to their segregation from core application logic. Isolation of components to remove dependencies is facilitated using mocks and spies that are documented in this chapter.

Chapter 9, A Brief Look at Testing Animations shows you how to test basic animations and delays synchronously and asynchronously. This is just an introduction into animations as AngularJS did a major overhaul on the animation aspect of their framework and the result included the mock.animate module.

What you need for this book

The recipes in this book use AngularJS version 1.2.x, available from the AngularJS website at `https://angularjs.org/`. Tests within recipes in this book use Jasmine version 2.0.x, available from the pivotal GitHub repository at `https://github.com/pivotal/jasmine/raw/master/dist/jasmine-standalone-2.0.0.zip`. You will need to include the angular.js.min and jasmine.js files in your project folders for your tests to work.

The code snippets shown in the book are just example snippets to support the explanations. Please refer to respective chapter files present in the code bundle for complete reference and understanding.

Who this book is for

AngularJS Testing Cookbook is for AngularJS developers who want to test their web applications developed using the framework. Developers with a basic comprehension of AngularJS and test-related concepts will find examples of how to test core components with the AngularJS framework, and server, the AngularJS framework, to form a foundation for further development.

Conventions

In this book, you will find a number of styles of text that distinguish between different kinds of information. Here are some examples of these styles, and an explanation of their meaning.

Code words in text are shown as follows: "The `expect` function takes a value that is matched against an `expected` value."

A block of code is set as follows:

```
it('should assign scope emcee to element text', function () {
  $scope.emcee = 'Izzy Ice';
  $scope.$digest();
  expect(element.text()).toBe('Step up Izzy Ice!');
});
```

When we wish to draw your attention to a particular part of a code block, the relevant lines or items are set in bold:

```
it('should assign scope emcee to element text', function () {
  $scope.emcee = 'Izzy Ice';
  $scope.$digest();
  expect(element.text()).toBe('Step up Izzy Ice!');
});
```

Any command-line input or output is written as follows:

```
npm install -g protractor
```

New terms and **important words** are shown in bold. Words that you see on the screen, in menus or dialog boxes for example, appear in the text like this: "clicking the **Next** button moves you to the next screen".

> Warnings or important notes appear in a box like this.

> Tips and tricks appear like this.

Reader feedback

Feedback from our readers is always welcome. Let us know what you think about this book—what you liked or may have disliked. Reader feedback is important for us to develop titles that you really get the most out of.

To send us general feedback, simply send an e-mail to feedback@packtpub.com, and mention the book title through the subject of your message.

If there is a book that you need and would like to see us publish, please send us a note in the **SUGGEST A TITLE** form on www.packtpub.com or e-mail suggest@packtpub.com.

If there is a topic that you have expertise in and you are interested in either writing or contributing to a book, see our author guide on www.packtpub.com/authors.

Customer support

Now that you are the proud owner of a Packt book, we have a number of things to help you to get the most from your purchase.

Downloading the example code

You can download the example code files for all Packt books you have purchased from your account at http://www.packtpub.com. If you purchased this book elsewhere, you can visit http://www.packtpub.com/support and register to have the files e-mailed directly to you.

Errata

Although we have taken every care to ensure the accuracy of our content, mistakes do happen. If you find a mistake in one of our books—maybe a mistake in the text or the code—we would be grateful if you would report this to us. By doing so, you can save other readers from frustration and help us improve subsequent versions of this book. If you find any errata, please report them by visiting http://www.packtpub.com/support, selecting your book, clicking on the **errata submission form** link, and entering the details of your errata. Once your errata are verified, your submission will be accepted and the errata will be uploaded to our website, or added to any list of existing errata, under the Errata section of that title.

Piracy

Piracy of copyright material on the Internet is an ongoing problem across all media. At Packt, we take the protection of our copyright and licenses very seriously. If you come across any illegal copies of our works, in any form, on the Internet, please provide us with the location address or website name immediately so that we can pursue a remedy.

Please contact us at copyright@packtpub.com with a link to the suspected pirated material.

We appreciate your help in protecting our authors, and our ability to bring you valuable content.

Questions

You can contact us at questions@packtpub.com if you are having a problem with any aspect of the book, and we will do our best to address it.

1

Setup and Configuration

In this chapter, you will learn the following recipes:

- ► Creating a basic AngularJS application
- ► Running a simple test using Jasmine
- ► Installing Protractor
- ► Running a simple test using Protractor
- ► Installing Karma
- ► Running tests using Karma
- ► Installing Testem
- ► Running tests using Testem
- ► Automating test runners using Grunt
- ► Automating test runners using Gulp

Introduction

In this chapter, you will learn various approaches available to configure and test an **AngularJS** application. These include simple unit tests using **Jasmine**, integration tests using **Protractor**, running tests using **Karma/Testem**, and finally using the **Grunt /Gulp** build tools to automate tasks.

It's important not to get too overwhelmed by automation of the various libraries available for testing. Each recipe within this book can simply be written and tested using Jasmine and Protractor. This cookbook's overall intention is to make each recipe as accessible as possible using the minimum number of toolsets.

The first half of this chapter is crucial to understand testing throughout this cookbook and we recommend that anyone looking to get started testing AngularJS applications reads it carefully.

There are, however, some great advantages to be gained from using some of the tools and libraries available out there to configure and automate running tests. The second half of this chapter will provide instructions on how to get started with these tools and the information learned from these recipes can be used throughout the book if you choose to.

Creating a basic AngularJS application

This recipe will form the structure for the majority of recipes throughout this cookbook. Additionally, it will provide a code base that can be used and tested in this chapter's recipes, sparing you the task of recreating your own code base throughout these initial configuration steps. The intention is for you, as a reader, to run recipes with minimal configuration and a limited set of libraries. The justification behind this simplicity is to maintain accessibility to each recipe independently. After completing this recipe, you will have a clear idea of the basic setup of an AngularJS application and can build on this foundation as the recipes advance.

Getting ready

Nothing specific is required for this recipe except your usual text editor and browser. Alternatively, you can use an online editor such as `http://jsfiddle.net` or `http://plnkr.co`.

How to do it...

1. You should first create a new directory to store the application files named `basic_example`.

2. Following this, create a new JavaScript file named `cookbook.js` and within this file, create an application module named `cookbook`:

   ```
   angular.module('cookbook', [])
   ```

3. Next, add the controller's constructor function to the module using the `.controller()` method. Assign a value to the `emcee` property on the `scope` instance:

   ```
   .controller('MainCtrl', ['$scope', function($scope) {
       $scope.emcee = 'Kool G Rap';
   }])
   ```

4. You now need to create an `index.html` file and add script references to both the `angular.js` source code (via their content delivery network) and the `cookbook.js` files either between the `<head>` tags or just before the closing `<body>` tag:

   ```
   <script type="text/javascript"
   src="http://code.angularjs.org/1.2.28/angular.min.js"></script>
   <script type="text/javascript" src="cookbook.js"></script>
   ```

5. Following this, bootstrap the application on a document level naming the module `cookbook`:

```
<html ng-app="cookbook">
```

6. Declare a controller named `MainCtrl` on an HTML `div` tag and using AngularJS's binding syntax, declare the `emcee` expression as follows:

```
<div ng-controller="MainCtrl">
  <span>Favourite member of the Juice Crew:
{{emcee}}</span>
</div>
```

This will be part of the HTML code, which you can see in its entirety, as follows:

```
<!DOCTYPE html>
<html ng-app="cookbook">
  <head>
    <script type="text/javascript"
    src="http://code.angularjs.org/1.2.28/angular.min.js">
    </script>
    <script type="text/javascript"
    src="cookbook.js"></script>
  </head>
  <body>
    <div ng-controller="MainCtrl">
      <span>Favourite member of the Juice Crew:
      {{emcee}}</span>
    </div>
  </body>
</html>
```

By this point, you may have created your application. You can see this by opening `index.html` in a browser. Also, `Kool G Rap` will be displayed as you can see in the following screenshot:

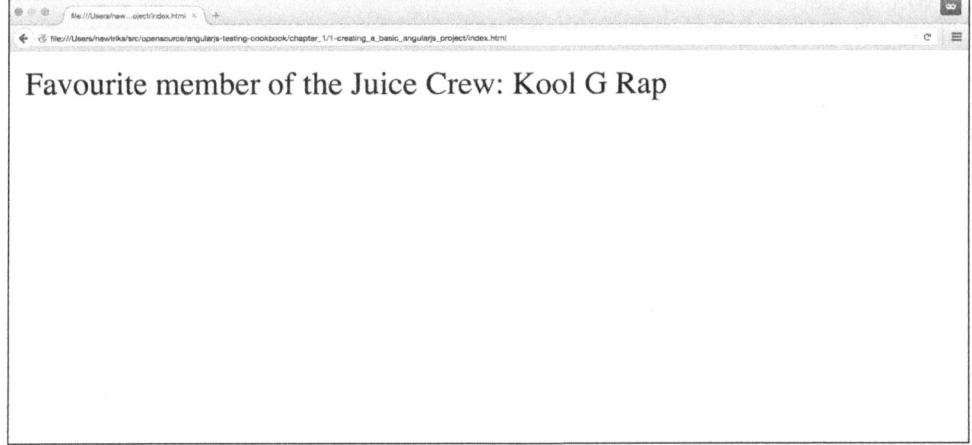

How it works...

The preceding process demonstrates the basic steps to configure a simple AngularJS application and should be familiar to you. The view component is automatically synchronized with the model data using AngularJS data binding. AngularJS takes data binding one step further by offering two-way data binding, resulting in changes to the model propagated to the view and vice versa.

See also

- ▶ For more information, specific to data binding, please consult the official documentation at `http://docs.angularjs.org/guide/databinding`.

- ▶ The AngularJS website offers a step-by-step tutorial available at `https://docs.angularjs.org/tutorial` that offers a quick overview to getting started.

Running a simple test using Jasmine

This book is focused on testing AngularJS with the behavior-driven development framework Jasmine. Jasmine is currently the framework used for testing the AngularJS code base. With the increased popularity of test runners and generators, the core basics of using Jasmine without these additional tools is sometimes overlooked. In this recipe, you will learn how to set up a basic specification, load an AngularJS module, instantiate a controller, and finally, run a spec testing a value on `scope`. The series of steps within this recipe are the basis for all your AngularJS tests using Jasmine. The general structure is as follows:

- ▶ Injecting dependencies
- ▶ Defining a context
- ▶ Writing specs

To solidify your base of comprehension regarding Jasmine, I recommend that you read through the documentation at `http://jasmine.github.io/2.0/introduction.html`. Within this recipe and throughout the rest of this book, we will follow the same directory structure as the AngularJS team (`https://github.com/angular/angular.js/tree/v1.2.28`). Their approach places application code within a directory named `src` and test-related code in a directory named `test`. You may have your own preferences on naming conventions and directory structure, and can choose to adopt those as you feel comfortable within the recipes throughout this book.

Getting ready

In this recipe, we will build upon the basic project created in this chapter's first recipe. To get ready, perform the following steps to install Jasmine and prepare your project for testing:

1. First, create a new directory called `src` in your project directory.

2. Next, move the `cookbook.js` file we wrote earlier in this chapter to the `src` directory.

3. Ensure that you have downloaded and unzipped the Jasmine framework by visiting `https://github.com/pivotal/jasmine/blob/master/dist/jasmine-standalone-2.0.0.zip?raw=true` in your browser.

4. Finally, copy the unzipped `jasmine-2.0.0` directory to a folder named `lib` within your project directory.

How to do it...

1. First, copy the `SpecRunner.html` file from the `jasmine-2.x.x` directory to a new directory named `test` in the project root folder.

2. Next, update the `SpecRunner.html` file with the correct paths to the Jasmine files:

```
<link rel="stylesheet" type="text/css"
href="../lib/jasmine-2.0.0/jasmine.css">
<script type="text/javascript" src="../lib/jasmine-
2.0.0/jasmine.js"></script>
<script type="text/javascript" src="../lib/jasmine-
2.0.0/jasmine-html.js"></script>
<script type="text/javascript" src="../lib/jasmine-
2.0.0/boot.js"></script>
```

3. Now, update the `SpecRunner.html` file to include AngularJS and AngularJS mock libraries. Order is important here, the `mocks.js` library must be below the AngularJS script include:

```
<script type="text/javascript" src="http://code.angularjs.
org/1.2.28/angular.js"></script>
<script type="text/javascript"
src="http://code.angularjs.org/1.2.28/angular-
mocks.js"></script>
```

4. Edit the `SpecRunner.html` file replacing the source file paths with our main `cookbook.js` file path:

```
<script type="text/javascript"
src="../src/cookbook.js"></script>
```

5. Next, create a new file named `cookbookSpec.js` within the test directory and add a `describe` block with a `beforeEach()` function that loads our module:

```
describe('MainCtrl', function () {
    beforeEach(module('cookbook'));
});
```

6. Still within the describe block, create a basic test that injects the `$controller` service and `$rootscope`. We can then create a new `$scope` object and instantiate a new instance of our controller providing the `$scope` object:

```
it('should assign the correct rapper to scope',
inject(function ($controller, $rootScope) {
  var $scope = $rootScope.$new();
  $controller('MainCtrl', {
    $scope: $scope
  });
}));
```

7. Create an expectation asserting that the value on scope is as expected:

```
expect($scope.emcee).toEqual('Kool G Rap');
```

8. Update `SpecRunner.html` to include `cookbookSpec.js`:

```
<script type="text/javascript"
src="cookbookSpec.js"></script>
```

9. Finally, open `SpecRunner.html` in a browser and you should see your first test passing:

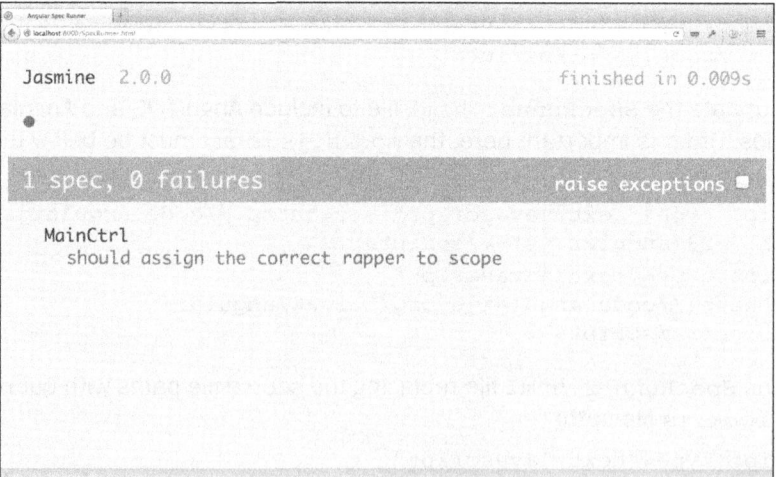

How it works...

In step 1, we use the `SpecRunner.html` file that Jasmine provides as a basis to build on for our test. Once we move the file into our directory structure, we need to ensure that all the paths correlate to the Jasmine files correctly; this we do in step 2.

The idea behind unit testing is to test the functionality of a piece of code in isolation. The AngularJS team helps to ease this process by offering replicas of objects called **mocks** that make unit testing easier by decoupling the components. The `angular-mocks.js` file loads the `ngMock` module (`https://docs.angularjs.org/api/ngMock`) so we can inject and mock AngularJS services. In step 3, we ensure that the AngularJS library is loaded in addition to the `angular-mocks.js` file.

 The `angular-mocks.js` library depends on AngularJS and therefore must be loaded after the `angular.js` file.

In step 4, we ensure that our main `cookbook.js` application code is loaded and ready to test. Then, in step 5, we define a context based on our `MainCtrl` controller and a `beforeEach()` function. The `beforeEach()` function is passed a string alias `cookbook` as an argument to the mock module function that configures information ready for the Angular injector.

In step 6, we define our test starting with the `it()` function that requires a string detailing our test intention, plus a second argument that makes use of the mock module's `inject` function. The mock inject function basically creates an injectable wrapper around this second argument creating a new instance of `$injector` for each test. The `$injector` instance is used to resolve all references for this recipe; this includes the `$controller service` function, which instantiates controllers and `$rootScope`. We use the injected `$rootScope` service to create a new child scope using the `$new()` method (`https://docs.angularjs.org/api/ng/type/$rootScope.Scope#$new`). This new child scope object is then passed to our newly instantiated controller that's constructed using the `$controller` service. Please refer to the introduction part of *Chapter 2, Getting Started with Testing and AngularJS* for further explanation about the Jasmine API.

Our expectation in step 7 is that when our `MainCtrl` controller is created, the scope's `emcee` property is expected to match the value of `Kool G Rap` (`https://github.com/pivotal/jasmine/wiki/Matchers`). This is asserted in step 7 by comparing the `$scope.emcee` property to `Kool G Rap`.

For a more in-depth overview of each of the steps involved in writing a test, including expectations and matchers, please read *Chapter 2, Getting Started with Testing and AngularJS*.

There's more...

An alternative approach to injecting the `controller` reference within the spec would be to move this logic and assign it to a variable reference outside of the spec. We can do this in another `beforeEach()` function with the refactored code looking like this:

```
describe('MainCtrl', function () {
  var mainCtrl, $scope;
  beforeEach(module('cookbook'));
  beforeEach(inject(function ($controller, $rootScope) {
    $scope = $rootScope.$new();
    $controller('MainCtrl', {
      $scope: $scope
    });
  }));
  it('should assign the correct rapper to scope', function () {
    expect($scope.emcee).toEqual('Kool G Rap');
  });
});
```

See also

  ▸ The *Creating a basic AngularJS application* recipe
  ▸ *Chapter 2, Getting Started with Testing and AngularJS*

Installing Protractor

During the first half of 2014, there was an abundance of renewed debate regarding **Test Driven Development** (**TDD**) taking place on the Web. David Heinemeier Hansson (creator of **Ruby on Rails**) challenged the fundamentals behind TDD and suggested placing more emphasis on system/browser tests. There are many arguments, for and against, as you can imagine, but what we are interested in is how we can implement the type of testing being advocated in an AngularJS application.

Luckily, to test application logic with browser tests (as opposed to the more granular unit tests), the AngularJS team developed a solution named Protractor (`https://github.com/angular/protractor`). This is a **Node.js** (`http://nodejs.org/`) program to run end-to-end tests against an actual browser using **WebDriver** (which you can access at `https://code.google.com/p/selenium/wiki/GettingStarted`). Webdriver is used to control browsers and simulate user actions. Protractor is quite an active project and therefore subject to change; this recipe is based on the current version at the time of writing this, which is 0.23.1. This recipe will focus on installing and configuring Protractor and Webdriver.

Getting ready

You will need to have Node.js (`http://nodejs.org/`) installed on your machine. For the purpose of this recipe, we use the Chrome browser that you can download at `http://www.google.co.uk/chrome/`. Alternative browsers can be configured and I recommend that you read the Protractor browser setup guide at `https://github.com/angular/protractor/blob/master/docs/browser-setup.md`.

How to do it...

1. You will first need to install Protractor using the `npm install -g protractor` command.

2. You will then need to install the necessary WebDrivers using the `webdriver-manager update` command.

3. Following this, start the **Selenium** server using the `webdriver-manager start` command.

4. Protractor will then accept a configuration file. Create a new file named `protractor.conf.js` with the following content:

```
exports.config = {
  seleniumAddress: 'http://localhost:4444/wd/hub',
  jasmineNodeOpts: {
    showColors: true, // use colors in the command line
    report
    defaultTimeoutInterval: 30000
  }
};
```

There's more...

Protractor can start an instance of the Selenium standalone server if you provide the path to the Selenium server standalone JAR as follows. This will slow down the overall time it takes to run your tests due to Protractor having to start the server as opposed to an instance already running:

```
seleniumServerJar: './node_modules/protractor/selenium/selenium-server-standalone-2.41.0.jar'
```

 The path may be vary based on OS or if you installed Protractor globally.

See also

▸ The *Running a simple test using Protractor* recipe

Running a simple test using Protractor

In the *Installing Protractor* recipe in this chapter, you learned how to configure Protractor and WebDriver. This recipe will introduce you to running a basic end-to-end test with Protractor. You will learn how to add test files to the Protractor configuration, add a basic end-to-end test, find DOM elements based on AngularJS attributes, and simulate user interaction. The latter has the potential to save a considerable amount of time testing your application and allows you to test expected user interaction. This sort of testing can prove indispensable and Protractor provides a simplified API to simulate user actions, as you will see within this recipe. Please refer to `https://github.com/angular/protractor/blob/master/docs/api.md` for a comprehensive list and explanation of the API methods available to you using Protractor.

Getting ready

Protractor will connect to a browser to run its tests. Preferably, we would want to run our application against an HTTP server and the quickest way to do this is using Python's (Version 2.4 or greater) **SimpleHTTPServer** by visiting `https://docs.python.org/2/library/simplehttpserver.html`.

 This is a cross-platform solution that requires Python to be installed on your machine. OS X, for example, will have this preinstalled while Windows users can install ActivePython or another Python installation route of your choice.

How to do it...

1. First, create a new directory and add a new file named `index.html` with the following content:

    ```
    <!DOCTYPE html>
    <html ng-app="cookbook">
      <head>
        <script
        src="https://code.angularjs.org/1.2.16/angular.js">
        </script>
        <script src="cookbook.js"></script>
      </head>
    ```

```
<body>
  <div ng-controller="MainCtrl">
    Favourite member of the Juice Crew: <input
    type="text" ng-model="emcee"><br>
    Emcee: <span ng-bind="emcee"></span>
  </div>
</body>
</html>
```

2. You then need to copy the `cookbook.js` file from the *Creating a basic AngularJS application* project recipe into the directory.

3. Following this, add a new file named `protractor.conf.js` with the following content:

```
exports.config = {
  seleniumAddress: 'http://localhost:4444/wd/hub',
  specs: ['cookbookSpec.js'],
  jasmineNodeOpts: {
    showColors: true,
    defaultTimeoutInterval: 30000
  }
};
```

4. You should then create a new file named `cookbookSpec.js` with the following content:

```
describe('favourite rapper', function () {
  it('should bind to input', function () {
    browser.get('');
    var emceeInput = element(by.model('emcee'));
    var emceeOutput = element(by.binding('emcee'));
    expect(emceeOutput.getText()).toBe('Kool G Rap');
    emceeInput.clear();
    emceeInput.sendKeys('Aesop Rock');
    expect(emceeOutput.getText()).toBe('Aesop Rock');
  });
});
```

5. Now, start the local HTTP server by running the `python -m SimpleHTTPServer` command (this command serves HTTP service on IP address `0.0.0.0` using port `8000` by default; you need to use `python -m http.server` if you are a windows user.) and the Selenium server with the `webdriver-manager start` command.

6. Once the server has started, in the command-line console of your choice, run the `protractor protractor.conf.js` command. As a result, you should see the following output:

```
Using the selenium server at http://localhost:4444/wd/hub
.

Finished in 3.204 seconds
1 test, 2 assertions, 0 failures
```

How it works...

In step 1, we create an HTML file, which is a basic AngularJS binding example. Step 3 shows the addition of a specs option that expects an array of relative filenames or a glob pattern. Step 4 executes the following sequence of events:

▸   The `should bind to input` spec begins using the Protractor global browser variable that is a wrapper around a WebDriver instance. The `get()` function expects a URL or path to a running web page for the AngularJS application. The web page can be run over a local web server, which we start in step 5.

▸   Search for elements on the page using the `element()` method and its additional AngularJS-specific strategies, for example binding names (`ng-bind` or `{{}}`) and elements by input using `ng-model`. The element method does not return a DOM element, but an ElementFinder. Calls to element can be chained to find child elements within a parent.

▸   Define an assertion based on the input field value. The initial value will be the default value assigned to the `$scope.emcee` property in the controller.

▸   Clear the input field value using the `clear()` method on the ElementFinder.

▸   Populate the input field using the `sendKeys()` method on the ElementFinder.

▸   Reassert, based on the updated input field, that the output binding has worked as expected.

The final steps run the local HTTP server and the Protractor tests displaying the results.

There's more...

A `baseUrl` option is available within the Protractor configuration, for example `baseUrl` (`http://0.0.0.0:8000`). This enables the use of relative paths using the `get ()` method that's available on Protractor's browser function, for example `browser.get();`. Please read the Protractor API documentation for more information on available functions (`http://angular.github.io/protractor/#/api?view=Protractor`).

There are some additional Chrome-specific options that can prove quite useful within your development toolkit. These can be added using a `chromeOptions` object; using this object will display the frame rate within your browser. Monitoring frame rate for consistency and a value between 30 to 60 frames per second (fps) can ensure that your application doesn't appear jerky and animations are smoothly run, for example:

```
capabilities: {
    'browserName': 'chrome',
    'chromeOptions': {
        'args': ['show-fps-counter=true']
    }
}
```

To target multiple spec files within your Protractor configuration, you can use a regular expression as opposed to an array of file names:

```
specs: ['test/*_spec.js']
```

See also

▸ The *Installing Protractor* recipe in this chapter

Installing Karma

This recipe will introduce you to the Karma test runner, which you can get at `http://karma-runner.github.io/`, for test-driven development and continuous integration. You will run through the basic process to install Karma version, which at time of writing this is 0.12.16.

Karma is another fantastic tool from the AngularJS team allowing you to execute JavaScript code in browsers. Earlier in this chapter, (in the *Running a simple test using Protractor* recipe in this chapter), you learned about Protractor, a tool for integration testing; what Karma offers is configuration for unit testing. It facilitates testing against multiple browsers, whether locally or on a continuous integration server. It can also be configured to run unit tests when application code changes via a watch feature. There are many plugins available to extend Karma and in this recipe we will use two of them. Firstly, we will use Jasmine throughout the cookbook so we will need the plugin from `https://github.com/karma-runner/karma-jasmine`. Secondly, we will run the tests in the Chrome browser using `https://github.com/karma-runner/karma-chrome-launcher`. Once you have completed this recipe, you'll have Karma installed with the Chrome and Jasmine plugins and ready to run some tests.

Getting ready

All you need is Node.js (`http://nodejs.org/`; ideally version 0.10.* or above) installed on your machine.

How to do it...

1. First, install Karma and the required plugins using the following command:

    ```
    npm install karma karma-jasmine karma-chrome-launcher --save-
    dev
    ```

2. Install the karma-cli to use Karma in your command line:

    ```
    npm install -g karma-cli.
    ```

3. Next, we use an option that some Node.js libraries provide to run initialization steps, which is typically called `init`. It guides us through the steps required to configure Karma on our command line:

    ```
    karma init
    ```

4. Now, at the prompt for testing framework, press *Enter* to accept the default option of **jasmine**.

5. Next, at the prompt to use Require.js, press *Enter* to accept the default option of **no**.

6. When you are prompted to automatically capture any browsers, press *Enter* twice to accept the default option of **Chrome**.

7. Next, at the prompt to define source file location, press *Enter* to accept the default option of an empty string.

8. At the prompt to define file patterns to exclude, press *Enter* to accept the default option of an empty string.

9. Finally, you will be prompted for Karma to watch for file changes so press Enter to accept the default option of **yes**.

The following screenshot shows you the steps discussed earlier:

```
simons-mbp-3:cookbook newtriks$ karma init

Which testing framework do you want to use ?
Press tab to list possible options. Enter to move to the next question.
> jasmine

Do you want to use Require.js ?
This will add Require.js plugin.
Press tab to list possible options. Enter to move to the next question.
> no

Do you want to capture any browsers automatically ?
Press tab to list possible options. Enter empty string to move to the next question.
> Chrome
>

What is the location of your source and test files ?
You can use glob patterns, eg. "js/*.js" or "test/**/*Spec.js".
Enter empty string to move to the next question.
>

Should any of the files included by the previous patterns be excluded ?
You can use glob patterns, eg. "**/*.swp".
Enter empty string to move to the next question.
>

Do you want Karma to watch all the files and run the tests on change ?
Press tab to list possible options.
> yes


Config file generated at "/Users/newtriks/src/cookbook/karma.conf.js".

simons-mbp-3:cookbook newtriks$ _
```

There's more...

If you prefer not to install karma-cli globally, allowing for different versions and different projects, you can remove the –g syntax. This will install the package to a `node_modules` folder within the root directory of the project:

npm install karma-cli

You can then run the commands from `node_modules`, as shown here:

./node_modules/.bin/karma init

See also

▶ The *Running a simple test using Karma* recipe

Running tests using Karma

To save time and effort when manually running your tests, you can use a test runner. The recipe, *Installing Karma*, gets you ready to run tests with Karma. This recipe will introduce you to automatically run a Jasmine test with Karma (which you can visit at http://karma-runner.github.io/). You will learn how to set up a basic configuration file and automatically run your tests with Karma.

Getting ready

You can either implement this as an initial step to an existing project, or build upon the basic project created in the first recipe. You can do this as follows:

1. Karma will need access to the angular.js and angular-mocks.js files, which can be downloaded from https://code.angularjs.org/1.2.28/. Ensure these are included in a lib/angular folder in your project root directory.

2. Copy the cookbook.js file from the recipe *Creating a basic AngularJS application*, into the src directory.

3. Finally, copy the cookbookSpec.js file from the *Running a simple test using Jasmine* recipe in this chapter, into a test directory.

How to do it...

Firstly, you need to create a Karma configuration file named karma.conf.js with the following code:

```
module.exports = function(config) {
  config.set({
    frameworks: ['jasmine'],
    files: [
        "lib/angular/angular.js",
        "lib/angular/angular-mocks.js",
        "src/cookbook.js",
        "test/cookbookSpec.js"
    ],
    autoWatch: true,
    browsers: ['Chrome']
  });
};
```

Once this has been created, you can run the following command:

```
karma start
```

As a result of this, you should see that Karma launches the Chrome browser and produces the following in the console window:

```
INFO [karma]: Karma v0.12.16 server started at http://localhost:9876/
INFO [launcher]: Starting browser Chrome
INFO [Chrome 35.0.1916 (Mac OS X 10.9.3)]: Connected on socket cZApYGrJWV7pGA_4u8-J with id 43420351
Chrome 35.0.1916 (Mac OS X 10.9.3): Executed 1 of 1 SUCCESS (0.025 secs / 0.023 secs)
```

How it works...

Karma requires a configuration file for it to run our AngularJS application tests. Let's step through the configuration options:

- ► `frameworks`: Framework adaptors that must be installed via the `karma init` process or manually, for example `npm install karma-jasmine --save-dev`.

- ► `files`: These are the file patterns specifying applications and test files.

- ► `autoWatch`: This option watches for changes to applications/test files and re-run tests.

- ► `browsers`: These are the launchers that must be installed via the `karma init` process or manually, for example `npm install karma-chrome-launcher --save-dev`.

The `angular.js` file is a dependency for `angular-mocks.js`, therefore `angular.js` must be declared before `angular-mocks.js`.

For a more comprehensive list of configuration options, please refer to Karma's configuration file documents at `http://karma-runner.github.io/0.12/config/configuration-file.html`.

There's more...

Use a glob pattern for files, as opposed to declaring each file explicitly, by inserting the following code:

```
files: [
  "lib/angular/angular.js",
  "lib/angular/angular-mocks.js",
  "src/**/*.js",
  "test/**/*.js"
]
```

See also

▸ The *Installing Karma* recipe in this chapter

Installing Testem

This recipe will introduce you to the **Testem** test runner (`https://github.com/airportyh/testem`) for test-driven-development and continuous integration. Testem is an alternative to Karma and although similar, it is favoured by some developers in the community including the **Lineman** (`https://github.com/linemanjs/lineman`) team. Karma and Testem have similar feature sets but Karma is developed with regular updates by the AngularJS team. As with Karma, Testem is framework-agnostic and configurable to run tests within a multitude of browsers, whether locally or on a Continuous Integration server. This recipe is based on the current version; at time of writing this it is 0.6.15 and will guide you on installing Testem.

Getting ready

You will need to have Node.js (`http://nodejs.org/`, version 0.10.* or greater) installed on your machine.

How to do it...

All you need to do is install Testem using the following command:

```
npm install testem --save-dev
```

You can then run the following command:

```
testem
```

You will see that Testem produces the following:

```
TEST'EM 'SCRIPTS!
Open the URL below in a browser to connect.
http://localhost:7357/

  Chrome 35.0
    0/0 ✔

No tests were run :(
```

See also

▸ The *Running a simple test using Testem* recipe

Running tests using Testem

To save time and effort manually running your tests, you can use a test runner. In the *Installing Testem* recipe you learned how to install and configure the runner. This recipe will introduce you to automatically running a Jasmine test with Testem within the Chrome browser. You will learn how to set up a basic configuration file and automatically run your tests.

Getting ready

To begin using Testem in this recipe you can either perform the following steps within an existing AngularJS project or build upon the basic project created in the first recipe:

1. Firstly, the `angular.js` and `angular-mocks.js` files need to be included. They can be downloaded from `https://code.angularjs.org/1.2.28/`. Ensure these are included in a `lib/angular` folder in your project root folder.

2. Copy the `cookbook.js` file from the *Creating a basic AngularJS application recipe* in this chapter, into the `src` directory.

3. Finally, copy the `cookbookSpec.js` file, from the *Running a simple test using Jasmine* recipe, into the `test` directory.

How to do it...

To start with, create a Testem configuration file named `testem.json` with the following JSON:

```
{
  "framework": "jasmine",
  "src_files": [
    "lib/angular/angular.js",
    "lib/angular/angular-mocks.js",
    "src/cookbook.js",
    "test/cookbookSpec.js"
  ],
  "launch_in_dev" : ["Chrome"]
}
```

Next, you need to run the `testem` command. As a result, you'll see that Testem launches the Chrome browser and our single test passing as shown in the following screenshot.

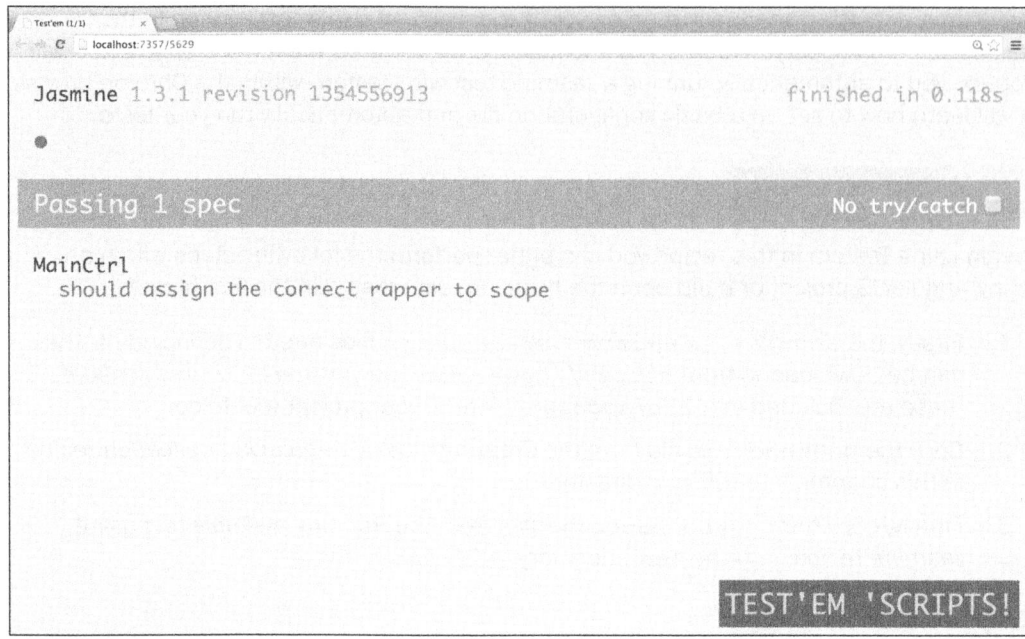

How it works...

A Testem configuration file allows finer control over what is included by the test runner. Let's step through the configuration options:

▶ `framework`: This is the test framework of choice. Testem already includes our preference of Jasmine.

▶ `src_files`: These are the file patterns specifying application and test files.

▶ `launch_in_dev`: This is the list of launchers to use for development runs.

The `angular.js` file is a dependency for `angular-mocks.js`, therefore `angular.js` must be declared before `angular-mocks.js`. Testem will automatically detect our files and changes made to the application or tests and rerun the tests.

For a more comprehensive list of configuration options, please refer to Testem's configuration file documents by visiting `https://github.com/airportyh/testem/blob/master/docs/config_file.md`.

There's more...

Use a glob pattern for files, as opposed to declaring each file explicitly, by inserting this:

```
"src_files": [
  "lib/angular/angular.js",
  "lib/angular/angular-mocks.js",
  "src/**/*.js",
  "test/**/*.js"
]
```

See also

▸ The *Installing Testem* recipe

Automating test runners using Grunt

The amount of tasks within an AngularJS-based project can rapidly increase, such as running an HTTP server, unit test runner, end-to-end test runner, or automating testing. These repetitive tasks can be automated using task runners such as **Grunt** (which you can download at `http://gruntjs.com/`), and **Gulp** (which can be downloaded at `http://gulpjs.com/`).

Grunt has been at the forefront of task runners for quite some time now; the community is vast with a great selection of available plugins. Grunt advises a global installation of its Command Line Interface (CLI) to access the grunt command anywhere on your system. Project and task configuration is contained within a Gruntfile, including the loading of plugins to extend the range of tasks available. A great starting point is on the Grunt website itself at `http://gruntjs.com/getting-started`. Armed with this basic knowledge, this recipe will focus on how to set up and configure Grunt to run the following tasks:

▸ HTTP web server

▸ Karma test runner

▸ WebDriver

▸ Protractor

Getting ready

You can either perform the following steps within an existing AngularJS project, or build upon the basic project created in the first recipe:

1. Firstly, the `angular.js` and `angular-mocks.js` files need to be included. They can be downloaded from `https://code.angularjs.org/1.2.28/`. Ensure these are included in a `lib/angular` folder in your project root folder.

2. Next, you then need to copy the `cookbook.js` file from the *Creating a basic AngularJS application* recipe into the `src` directory.

3. Next, copy the `cookbookSpec.js` file from the *Running a simple test using Jasmine* recipe into the `test/unit` directory.

4. Next, copy the `cookbookSpec.js` file from the *Running a simple test using Protractor* recipe into the `test/e2e` directory.

5. Finally, you need to ensure that you have installed Protractor globally, that is using the `-g` lag (please refer to the *Installing Protractor* recipe in this chapter to see how to do this). Also ensure that the Selenium standalone server has been downloaded and installed.

Once Protractor and the Selenium server have both been installed, you are now ready to begin.

How to do it...

1. First, let's install the Grunt CLI globally using this command:

```
npm install -g grunt-cli
```

2. Next, run the following command to interactively create a `package.json` file and either add your specific configuration or accept the defaults when prompted:

```
npm init
```

3. Following this, install the rest of the dependencies required for this recipe locally:

```
npm install grunt grunt-contrib-connect grunt-karma grunt-
protractor-runner grunt-protractor-webdriver karma karma-
chrome-launcher karma-jasmine load-grunt-tasks 0.4.0—save-dev
```

4. Now, install the WebDrivers using Protractor by running this command:

```
/node_modules/protractor/bin/webdriver-manager update
```

5. A Karma configuration file named `karma.conf.js` can then be created with the following code:

```
module.exports = function(config) {
  config.set({
    frameworks: ['jasmine'],
    files: [
        "lib/angular/angular.js",
        "lib/angular/angular-mocks.js",
        "src/cookbook.js",
        "test/unit/cookbookSpec.js"
    ],
    autoWatch: true,
    browsers: ['Chrome']
  });
};
```

6. You should then create a Protractor configuration file named `protractor.conf.js`, which contains the following code:

```
exports.config = {
  seleniumAddress: 'http://localhost:4444/wd/hub',
  jasmineNodeOpts: {
    showColors: true,
    defaultTimeoutInterval: 30000
  }
};
```

7. Next, another file named `Gruntfile.js` needs to be created, which will be in the root of the project directory with the following code:

```
module.exports = function (grunt) {
  require('load-grunt-tasks')(grunt);
  grunt.initConfig({
    connect: {
      server: {
        options: {
          port: 8000,
          base: 'src'
        }
      }
    },
    karma: {
      unit: {
        configFile: 'karma.conf.js'
      }
    },
    protractor: {
      e2e: {
        options: {
          args: {
            specs: ['test/e2e/cookbookSpec.js']
          },
          configFile: 'protractor.conf.js',
          keepAlive: true
        }
      }
    },
    protractor_webdriver: {
      start: {
        options: {
          path: './node_modules/protractor/bin/',
          command: 'webdriver-manager start',
```

```
        },
      }
    }
  });
  grunt.registerTask('test', [
    'karma:unit'
  ]);
  grunt.registerTask('e2e', [
    'connect:server',
    'protractor_webdriver:start',
    'protractor:e2e'
  ]);
}
```

8. Finally, you can run the unit tests of Karma using `grunt test`. You can then run the end-to-end tests of Protractor using `grunt e2e`.

How it works...

Step 1 simply runs the global installation for `grunt-cli` (which you can download at `https://github.com/gruntjs/grunt-cli`). This enables us to access the Grunt command anywhere on our system. Step 2 and step 3 install all of the dependencies required to successfully run all the Grunt tasks.

After this, step 4 and step 5 show how to set up the configuration files for both Karma and Protractor defining our unit and end-to-end specs.

>  Using the `grunt-karma` command, you can eliminate the need for a `karma.conf` configuration file and define the configuration in the Gruntfile instead. Visit `https://github.com/karma-runner/grunt-karma#heres-an-example-that-puts-the-config-in-the-gruntfile` to discover more.

In step 6, we see the `Gruntfile.js` file where we define all the necessary tasks to automate the unit and end-to-end tests. Both work by:

- **Unit tests**: Running the unit tests with Karma is relatively straightforward and simply requires the `grunt-karma` plugin (`https://github.com/karma-runner/grunt-karma`). We then add a `karma` target and provide the `configFile` created in step 4. Finally, we register a task with Grunt named `test`, which calls `karma:unit` and runs the unit tests.

The `grunt-karma` module supports configuring options for multiple targets, for example **dev** (development) and **continuous** (Continuous Integration). To use the continuous integration mode, use the `singleRun` option. In development, we can use the `autoWatch` option.

For Continuous Integration option, use the following code:

```
{
  singleRun: true,
  browsers: ['PhantomJS']
},
```

For Development option, use the following code:

```
{
  autoWatch: true
}
```

▶ **End-to-end tests**: Running the end-to-end tests with Protractor is slightly more complex due to the additional requirement of running HTTP and Selenium servers. We can run Protractor using the `grunt-protractor-runner` plugin (`https://github.com/teerapap/grunt-protractor-runner`) and adding a `protractor` target. Within the `protractor` target, we create an `e2e` target and a single option configuration file pointing to our `protractor.conf.js` file that we created in step 5. The `grunt-protractor-webdriver` plugin (which you can download at `https://github.com/seckardt/grunt-protractor-webdriver`) enables us to start the WebDriver that we define as a sole command in the `protractor_webdriver` `e2e` target. To start a local HTTP server, we use the `grunt-contrib-connect` plugin (`https://github.com/gruntjs/grunt-contrib-connect`) with three options, mainly port, hostname, and the base path, which is the `src` directory containing our AngularJS application. Finally, we register a task with Grunt named `e2e` that connects to our web server, starts the Selenium standalone server, and runs Protractor, phew!

Finally, to run all of these tasks, we call either the `test` or `e2e` task.

See also

▶ The *Automating test runners using Gulp* recipe

▶ Brunch (`http://brunch.io/`)

Automating test runners using Gulp

An additional task runner you can use, other than Grunt, is Gulp (you can download it at `http://gulpjs.com/`). Gulp is a stream-based build system with a simple yet powerful API focusing on code over configuration. Gulp builds use the Node.js streams that do not need to write temporary files or folders to disk, which results in faster builds. I advise you to read this excellent article on streams at `https://github.com/substack/stream-handbook`. The Gulp API is small and extremely simple:

- ▸ `gulp.src(globs[, options])`: This returns a readable stream
- ▸ `gulp.dest(path)`: This can receive an input stream and output to a destination, for example, writing files
- ▸ `gulp.task(name[, deps], fn)`: This defines tasks using orchestrator (`https://github.com/orchestrator/orchestrator`)
- ▸ `gulp.watch(glob [, opts], tasks)` or `gulp.watch(glob [, opts, cb])`: This enables watching for file changes and then running a task or tasks when changes are detected

Please visit `https://github.com/gulpjs/gulp/blob/master/docs/API.md` for an explanation of the API.

Gulp has its own configuration file called a **Gulpfile**, focused on code over configuration. It offers a coherent read with a clear visualization of flow. Gulp discourages the use of writing plugins for tasks that don't require a dedicated plugin focusing on providing streams and basic tasks. This recipe will focus on how to set up and configure Gulp to run the following tasks:

- ▸ HTTP web server
- ▸ Karma test runner
- ▸ WebDriver
- ▸ Protractor

Getting ready

You can either implement this as an initial step to an existing project or build upon the basic project created in the first recipe. If integrating into an existing project, ensure that you have specified the correct source and test files with their corresponding paths. Once configured, Gulp will run your tests as expected. If using the cookbook example project, then follow these steps:

1. Firstly, `angular.js` and `angular-mocks.js` files need to be included. They can be downloaded from `https://code.angularjs.org/1.2.28/`. Ensure these are included in a `lib/angular` folder in your project root folder.

2. You then need to copy the `cookbook.js` file created in the *Creating a basic AngularJS application* recipe into the `src` directory.

3. Finally, copy the `cookbookSpec.js` file from the *Running a simple test using Jasmine* recipe in this chapter into a `test/unit` directory.

4. To prepare yourself completely for this recipe, you can then copy the `cookbookSpec.js` file from the *Running a simple test using Protractor* recipe into a `test/e2e` directory.

How to do it...

1. First, let's install Gulp and Protractor globally using this command:

```
npm install -g gulp protractor
```

2. Next, run the following command to interactively create a `package.json` file and either add your specific configuration or accept the defaults when prompted:

```
npm init
```

3. Following this, install the rest of the dependencies required for this recipe locally:

```
npm install connect gulp-load-plugins gulp-protractor karma karma-chrome-launcher karma-jasmine -—save-dev
```

4. You then need to create a Karma configuration file named `karma.conf.js` with the following code:

```
module.exports = function () {
    return {
        frameworks: ['jasmine'],
        files: [
            "lib/angular/angular.js",
            "lib/angular/angular-mocks.js",
            "src/cookbook.js",
            "test/unit/cookbookSpec.js"
        ],
        autoWatch: true,
        browsers: ['Chrome']
    };
};
```

5. Create a Protractor configuration file named `protractor.conf.js` with the following code:

```
exports.config = {
  seleniumServerJar:
  './node_modules/protractor/selenium/selenium-server-
  standalone-2.41.0.jar',
  specs: ['test/e2e/cookbookSpec.js'],
  jasmineNodeOpts: {
    showColors: true,
```

```
        defaultTimeoutInterval: 30000
    }
};
```

6. Following this, create a file named `gulpfile.js` in the root of the project directory with the following code:

```
var gulp = require('gulp');
var $ = require('gulp-load-plugins')();

gulp.task('webdriver_update', $.protractor.webdriver_update);

gulp.task('connect', function () {
  var connect = require('connect');
  var app = connect()
    .use(connect.static('src'));

  $.server = require('http').createServer(app)
    .listen(8000);
});

gulp.task('test', function (done) {
  var karma = require('karma').server;
  var karmaConf = require('./karma.conf.js')();
  karma.start(karmaConf, done);
});

gulp.task('e2e', ['connect', 'webdriver_update'], function (done)
{
  gulp.src(['test/e2e/cookbookSpec.js'])
    .pipe($.protractor.protractor({
      configFile: './protractor.conf.js',
    }))
    .on('end', function () {
      $.server.close();
      done();
    });
});
```

7. Finally, you can start the testing! You can run unit tests with Karma using `gulp test` and run the end-to-end tests with Protractor using `gulp e2e`.

How it works...

Step 1 and step 2 install all the dependencies required to successfully run all of the Gulp tasks. Step 3 and step 4 show how we can set up the configuration files for both Karma and Protractor defining our unit and end-to-end specifications.

Step 5 has the `gulpfile.js` file where we define all the necessary tasks to automate the unit and end-to-end tests:

- **Unit tests**: As opposed to the approach taken in the *Automating test runners using Grunt* recipe, a dedicated plugin to run Karma is not really necessary. We simply call the `start()` function, providing the `configFile` created in step 4 as the first argument, and the Gulp callback to cleanly exit the task as necessary. Finally, we register a task with Gulp named `test` that calls the Karma test runner to the unit tests.

 To set a default task as opposed to defining the task name explicitly, add the following line of code to your gulp file:

```
gulp.task('default', ['test']);
```

- **End-to-end tests**: End-to-end tests need to run Protractor but also have the additional tasks of running HTTP and Selenium servers. We can run Protractor using the `gulp-protractor` plugin (`https://github.com/mllrsohn/gulp-protractor`). The connect task sets up a static HTTP server on port 8000 using the files within the `src` directory. Also, the `webdriver_update` task uses the `webdriver-manager` script included with Protractor to ensure that necessary drivers are installed; if not, then they will automatically get installed. This is a slight overhead each time the `e2e` task is run. However, it can easily be removed and you can call the gulp task independently if required. Within the actual `e2e` task, we pass the path to the test files to gulp's `src` function. We can then stream the file structure to the gulp-protractor `protractor()` function, including the `protractor.conf.js` file created in step 5 as an additional option. Listening for the end event, a handler will close the static HTTP server and then ensure the gulp callback is called to complete the set of events.

Finally, to run these tasks, we call either the `test` task or the `e2e` target.

See also

- The *Automating test runners using Grunt* recipe
- An exceptional resource for learning about streams is the Streams Handbook (which you can access at `https://github.com/substack/stream-handbook`)

2
Getting Started with Testing and AngularJS

In this chapter, you will learn the following recipes:

- ▶ Loading a module
- ▶ Writing a test spec
- ▶ Debugging AngularJS code
- ▶ Mocking injected instances using an object
- ▶ Mocking injected instances using spies

Introduction

This chapter explains the principles required to test AngularJS code using Jasmine. This book focuses on using Jasmine, however, there are also other great options available for testing AngularJS code including **Mocha** (`http://mochajs.org`). Specifics detailed within this chapter are crucial to get a test running, for example, dependency injection and registering modules. This chapter will repeatedly reinforce familiar recurrent patterns typical to testing and will become second nature throughout the rest of the book. After discovering the core essentials required when running a test, the remaining recipes will guide you to dig deeper into debugging your code both in your application and tests. Dependency injection allows us to test code in isolation with stubs/spies and mocks that we will cover later in this chapter. Jasmine uses **Behavior-Driven Development** (**BDD**) solution that Dan North developed based on **Test-Driven Development** (**TDD**). BDD offers developer's guidelines for the process of testing based on the concept of user stories. The process follows a pattern:

- ▶ `given`: There first needs to be an initial context defined. In Jasmine we would use the describe function, for example:

  ```
  describe("Signup form", function(){});)
  ```

- ▶ `when`: This is used to denote an event occurrence; in Jasmine we would use another describe function nested in the given context, for example:

  ```
  describe("Signup form", function(){
  describe("when the submit button is clicked", function(){});)
  });)
  ```

- ▶ `then`: This ensures an outcome; in Jasmine we would use the if function, for example:

  ```
  if("should validate the form", function(){});)
  ```

Jasmine will take the title values we provide in the `describe()` and `it()` functions and integrate them into the final output displayed on completion of our test. It is important to be clear and concise with the titles, in order to ensure what we are testing is easy to interpret.

Test methods require a *clean slate* to ensure that each test is run in isolation from other setup-related tasks. When testing AngularJS applications, the required modules need to be loaded, directives need their associated elements to be compiled, and the scope needs to be recreated. These, along with many other characteristics specific to configuring AngularJS modules, ensure that each test is independently configured.

It's likely you will need more than one test for your AngularJS components. As you add further tests you'll find duplication will inevitably occur based on configuration of the component. To help reduce this duplication, common logic can be extracted out into two Jasmine helper functions: `beforeEach` which runs before each test and `afterEach` which runs after. These are perfect for abstracting duplicate code out of the tests themselves and help us adhere to the **Don't Repeat Yourself** (**DRY**) principle, reducing repetition.

Loading a module

AngularJS uses modules to contain the different parts of the application such as controllers, services, filters, and so on. To test these distinct parts, we first need a reference to applications associated module and we need to load it. An AngularJS module is configured in preparation to inject using the ngMock module (`https://code.angularjs.org/1.2.28/docs/api/ngMock`). The ngMock module enables us to inject and mock AngularJS services into unit tests. The ngMock module exposes an `angular.mock.module` function that also has the abbreviated version available on the window named `module`. This recipe will demonstrate how to configure a module ready for injection and therefore enables us to test the specific components within an AngularJS application.

Getting ready

All that is required for this recipe is a simple AngularJS application bootstrapping a component. For this recipe, I will use a service but you can replace this with any component of your choice such as a directive. The ngMock module is provided in a file named `angular-mocks.js`. This, along with the `angular.js` file is required to be included in your project. Both files can be downloaded from `https://code.angularjs.org/1.2.28/`. Please refer to the *Running a simple test using Jasmine* recipe in *Chapter 1, Setup and Configuration*, to understand how these files are included in your codebase.

How to do it...

Typically, the `angular.mock.module` function is used within a `beforeEach` function. The `module` function expects either a module string alias or an object literal to replace the string, which will be also injected:

1. First, let's look at using a string alias:

   ```
   beforeEach(module('services.emcees'));
   ```

2. Next, we use an object literal, as follows:

   ```
   beforeEach(module('services.emcees', {
     'beatjunkies': {
       'dj': 'Babu'
     }
   }));
   ```

3. Following on, you can now retrieve the resolved object within your test using the `beatjunkies` reference, which will return the object `{'dj': 'Babu'}`.

4. Lastly, you can also provide a function that will provide the rapper reference, as follows:

   ```
   beforeEach(module('cookbook', {
     'beatjunkies': {
       'dj': 'Babu'
     }
   }, function ($provide) {
     $provide.value('rapper', 'madchild');
   }));
   ```

There's more...

To configure multiple modules, all you need to do is simply add each module, separating them with a comma. Here's an example of a `beforeEach` function:

```
beforeEach(module('services.emcees', 'services.deejays',
'services.breakers'));
```

 Please be aware that you cannot load a module after injection has taken place.

I recommend that you take a look at the fantastic angular-debaser library available at `http://decipherinc.github.io/angular-debaser` to help manage your fixtures as they grow.

Writing a test spec

Using the global Jasmine function called `it`, we can define our spec that includes the title and a function containing the spec code. When unit testing, as opposed to end-to-end testing, I follow the rule of **one expectation per spec**. This rule focuses the spec onto one area of functionality and helps clarify what is either successfully working as expected or on the other hand, failing. The drawback of this approach is that it involves writing more code. This recipe will provide you with an example spec for a directive, demonstrating how to update the scope and then assert a value within the DOM element.

Getting ready

For this example, I will test against a directive that updates the element text content based on a scope value. This value is assigned when a method on scope named `onClick` is triggered. This could have been called by a button click in the HTML, for example. Here is an example directive to be used in this test:

```
.directive('emcee', function () {
  return {
    restrict: 'E',
    link: function (scope, element) {
      scope.onClick = function() {
        element.text('Step up ' + scope.emcee + '!');
      };
    }
  };
});
```

Both the `angular.js` and `angular-mocks.js` files are required to be included in your project and can be downloaded from `https://code.angularjs.org/1.2.28/`. Please refer to the *Running a simple test using Jasmine* recipe in *Chapter 1, Setup and Configuration* to understand how these files are included in your code base.

How to do it...

1. First, create two variables. One for scope (`var scope`) and another for our element (`var element`).

2. Ensure you load your module: `beforeEach(module('cookbook'));`.

3. Create a `beforeEach` function to inject the necessary dependencies and assign them to the variables declared in step 1, including creating new scope object and assign our `emcee` value to the scope:

   ```
   beforeEach(inject(function ($rootScope, $compile) {
     rootScope = $rootScope;
     scope = $rootScope.$new();
       scope.emcee = 'Izzy Ice';
   }));
   ```

4. Next, within the `beforeEach` function from step 3, add the following to create and compile our directive:

   ```
   element = angular.element('<emcee></emcee>');
   $compile(element)(scope);
   ```

5. Next, still within the `beforeEach` function from step 3, process all of the watchers:

   ```
   scope.$digest();
   ```

6. You need to create a new spec defining what the expected outcome of this test is. An example is shown here:

   ```
   it('should assign scope emcee to element text when the
   onClick handler is called', function () {});
   ```

7. Now, within the spec from step 6, add the following to trigger the `onClick` method defined in the scope:

   ```
   scope.onClick();
   ```

8. Still within the spec from step 6, add an expectation that the element text matches our expected value:

   ```
   expect(element.text()).toBe('Step up Izzy Ice!');
   ```

9. The final spec should look as follows and we can now expect that running this test will result in Jasmine displaying that the test passes:

```
it('should assign scope emcee to element text when the onClick
handler is called', function () {
  scope.onClick ();
  expect(element.text()).toBe('Step up Izzy Ice!');
});
```

How it works...

In step 1, we declare some convenience variables to be reused throughout all tests. These variables get assigned in step 3 using a `beforeEach` function that ensures that the values assigned are reset before each test is run. In step 3, we also assign a value to `scope.emcee` and expect this value to be concatenated by our directive. In step 4, we create and compile our directive (for more information on this please refer to the *Starting with Testing Directives* recipe in *Chapter 5, Testing User Interaction and Directives*). In step 5, we call `scope.$digest()` function to ensure that all of the AngularJS bindings are updated.

The test spec is declared in step 6 and states what we expect from this test. In step 7, we call the `onClick()` method and then update the element text with the value provided on the scope. The AngularJS element provides the convenience `text` method that returns the text content of the element. The expectation in step 8 uses the value returned from the text method to be compared against our expected value `Step up Izzy Ice` using the `toBe` matcher.

There's more...

Matchers, along with expectations, form the foundation of all your tests, and together follow the same simple sequence—*I expect this to match that*. Matchers, as with expectations, remain the same functionally regardless of whether you use AngularJS or not. A matcher implements a Boolean comparison between the actual value and the expected value. There are a wide array of matchers to suit the specific expectation you're testing and they can all be reviewed at `https://github.com/pivotal/jasmine/wiki/Matchers`.

Here is a list of some commonly used matchers:

▶ This will pass if the actual value contains expected value:

```
expect($djListItems().eq(0).html()).toContain('D-
Styles<br>\nQbert<br>\nMix Master
Mike<br>\nShortkut<br>\nA-Trak<br>\nBabu');
```

▶ This will pass if the actual value and expected value are the same object (uses === for equality):

```
expect(element.text()).toBe('Izzy Ice');
```

- This will pass if the actual value and expected value are equivalent (uses == for equality):

  ```
  expect(scope.emcees.length).toEqual(7);
  ```

- This will pass if the actual value matches expected string or regular expression:

  ```
  expect(element.text()).toMatch(/Eyedea/);
  ```

- This will pass if the actual value is defined:

  ```
  expect($cookies.bboy).toBeDefined();
  ```

- This will pass if actual value is not defined:

  ```
  expect($cookies.writer).not.toBeDefined();
  ```

- This will pass if the actual value is null:

  ```
  expect(BreakBeat.tracks()).toBeNull();
  ```

- This will pass if the actual value is not null:

  ```
  expect(Scratch.tracks()).not.toBeNull();
  ```

- This will pass if the actual value is false:

  ```
  expect(element(by.css('button')).getAttribute('disabled')).
  toBeFalsy();
  ```

- This will pass if the actual value is true:

  ```
  expect(angular.element(element.find('a')[0])
  .parent().hasClass('ng-
  hide')).getAttribute('disabled')).toBeTruthy();
  ```

- This will pass if the actual value is less than expected value:

  ```
  expect(scope.deejays.length).toBeLessThan(2);
  ```

- This will pass if the actual value is greater than expected value:

  ```
  expect(scope.bboys.length).toBeGreaterThan(4);
  ```

Debugging AngularJS code

There will potentially be a time when you need to dig a little deeper into your code when something isn't responding the way you expect. There are a variety of options available to us to help gain a more comprehensive understanding of the sequence of events that will take place when our application is run. This recipe will demonstrate the available methods to debug your AngularJS code to help diagnose obstacles that you may face when testing.

Getting ready

For this recipe, you simply need some AngularJS code running to test various debugging options. You can use the code from the *Writing a test spec* recipe in this chapter.

How to do it...

1. First, let's use the simplest available option, which is the `$log` service as it will write messages to the browser console. Include the `$log` service and then write to the console log using `$log.debug('message')`. The available methods are: `log`, `warn`, `info`, `debug` and `error`. The default is to log debug messages, and you can disable this using `$logProvider.debugEnabled(false);`.

2. Next, let's use the `debugger` statement to suspend the browser at a specific point of execution. Navigate to a specific point in your code and add the `debugger;` statement. The `debugger;` statement suspends execution and is similar to setting a breakpoint in your code. If your browser supports the statement, then on reload you should be able to navigate through the call stack in your browser console.

3. Following this, we can actually interact with the scope of an element in the browser console by first retrieving an element using the document `querySelector` method and then wrapping the result in the AngularJS element function. We can also follow similar logic to debug services where the element is the DOM node and ngApp was defined. You can try running the following commands and analyzing the output:

    ```
    var element = document.querySelector('.css-selector');
    var elementScope = angular.element(element).scope();
    element = document.querySelector('html');
    var service =
    angular.element(document).injector().get('emcees');
    ```

    Your output should now look like this:

```
Favourite member of the Juice Crew: Kool G Rap

Q   Elements  Network  Sources  Timeline  Profiles  Resources  Audits | Console | AngularJS
⊘  ▽  <top frame>                    ▼
> var element = document.querySelector('span');
  undefined
> var elementScope = angular.element(element).scope();
  undefined
> elementScope
  ▶ ChildScope {$id: "003", this: ChildScope, $$listeners: Object, $$listenerCount: Object, $parent: Scope...}
> var element = document.querySelector('html');
  undefined
> var service = angular.element(element).injector().get('emcees');
  undefined
> service
  ▶ Object {get: function}
> $scope
  ▶ ChildScope {$id: "003", this: ChildScope, $$listeners: Object, $$listenerCount: Object, $parent: Scope...}
>
```

4. Finally, take a look at **Batarang**, the WebInspector extension for Chrome from the Angular team. Go ahead and follow the installation instructions on the Github repository page at `https://github.com/angular/angularjs-batarang` and read through some of the tutorials that they provide. Targeting an element, as seen in step 3, can be now simplified using Batarang by first inspecting the element and then typing `$scope` into the console.

See also

▸ You can check out another great tool: ng-inspector (`http://ng-inspector.org/`).

▸ A Google engineer named Addy Osmani has frequently produced great examples of how to debug your code with a specific focus on the Chrome DevTools. I recommend that you follow his Twitter feed at `http://www.addyosmani.com/blog/tag/devtools`, where he highlights many valuable tips.

Mocking injected instances using an object

In the ideal world, as a developer, you would want to ensure your code is loosely coupled. As your application grows, so do the dependencies and therefore the testing can get difficult and thus become less maintainable. Imitating or faking dependencies is known as mocking and facilitates the isolation of test modules while making it generally easier to test. We can very simply mock a dependency with an object and register it with the injector using the AngularJS `$provide` service; this recipe will demonstrate how it can be done.

Getting ready

In this example, a factory called *Artists* is the module under test and the `imageStore` factory is its only dependency. The Artists factory exposes an object with the thumb method that expects an `id` value as its sole argument. The `imageStore` dependency is expected to expose a `thumbnailUrl` method and using an `id` value returns the thumbnail URL:

```
angular.module('artists', [])
  .factory('Artists', ['imageStore',
    function (imageStore) {
      // API
      return {
        thumb: function (id) {
          return imageStore.thumbnailUrl(id);
        }
      };
    }
  ]);
```

Both the `angular.js` and `angular-mocks.js` files are required to be included in your project and can be downloaded from `https://code.angularjs.org/1.2.28/`. Please refer to the *Running a simple test using jasmine* recipe in *Chapter 1, Setup and Configuration*, to understand how these files are included in your code base.

How to do it...

Once you have a module and a `factory` defined, you are ready to begin with the test logic:

1. First, create a reference to the URL soon to be captured within our mock and a variable for the `Artists` injected instance:

   ```
   var url;
   var Artists;
   ```

2. Following this, register the mock factory ready for injection within a `beforeEach` function using the `$provide` service. Mock the `thumbnailUrl` function using an object. The `thumbnailUrl` function expects an `id` value and now we need to mock its behavior and assign the `url` variable with a concatenated string including the `id` parameter:

   ```
   beforeEach(module(function ($provide) {
     $provide.value('imageStore', {
       thumbnailUrl: function (id) {
         url = '/thumbs/' + id;
       }
     });
   }));
   ```

3. Next, run the `inject` method and using the `$injector` service, retrieve our Artists factory instance and assign it to a variable so that we can reuse it in our test:

   ```
   beforeEach(inject(function ($injector) {
     Artists = $injector.get('Artists');
   }));
   ```

4. Finally, create a simple test that will call the `Artists.thumb` function with an `id` value of `1` and write an expectation on the returned URL:

   ```
   it('return the correct artist thumbnailUrl', function () {
     Artists.thumb('1');
     expect(url).toBe('/thumbs/1');
   });
   ```

5. To conclude this recipe, here is the complete test example using the previous steps that mock out the `imageStore` using `$provide`. This will return an object defining the `thumbnailUrl` function, which will then concatenate the `id` argument with a string and assign it to the `url` variable. The test will then expect the URL to match the `'/thumbs/1'` value:

```
describe('Factory: artists', function () {
  var url;
  var Artists;

  beforeEach(module('artists'));

  beforeEach(module(function ($provide) {
    $provide.value('imageStore', {
      thumbnailUrl: function (id) {
        url = '/thumbs/' + id;
      }
    });
  }));

  beforeEach(inject(function ($injector) {
    Artists = $injector.get('Artists');
  }));

  it('return the correct artist thumbnailUrl',function () {
    Artists.thumb('1');
    expect(url).toBe('/thumbs/1');
  });
});
```

How it works...

The main logic is within step 2, where we use the `$provide` service's `value()` method (`https://docs.angularjs.org/api/auto/service/$provide`) that registers the `imageStore` mock factory object with the `$injector` service. The `$injector` service uses this mock object as a replacement of the `imageStore` with the associated fake result to the URL variable.

As you can see, we have easily replicated the logic of the `imageStore` object without having to reproduce all the unnecessary logic that the component may also provide, simply to run our tests specific to the Artists factory. This has therefore reduced our dependency on the `imageStore` factory and ensured that our test is run in isolation.

See also

> ▸ The *Mocking injected instances using spies* recipe in this chapter
>
> ▸ *Chapter 3, How to Test Navigation and Routing*

Mocking injected instances using spies

In the *Mocking injected instances using an object* recipe in this chapter, we stated that if the module you're testing has other module dependencies, you need to maintain isolation, as well as ensure that they are resolved appropriately. Jasmine provides functions called **spies** (`http://jasmine.github.io/2.0/introduction.html#section-Spies`). Spies are used by tests to imitate to be functions or objects and offer the ability to then track calls made to the spy, plus query arguments that may also have been provided. They have their own set of special matchers that enhance testing against expectations. This additional set of features augment our testing capabilities offering a greater range of expectations than normally available without spies. Once you understand the concept behind Jasmine spies, you will realize they are a powerful tool to use within your tests. To further enhance Jasmine spies, I recommend that you look at the Sinon.JS library (`http://sinonjs.org/`). This recipe will demonstrate how to mock an injected dependency using a Jasmine spy.

Getting ready

To help demonstrate the issue of injection dependency, I will provide an example module and spec:

1. First, let's take a look at this example module with two factories. Note that the second factory, named `scratch`, is used in the `deejays` factory:

```
angular.module('hiphop', [])
  .factory('deejays', function ($rootScope, scratch) {
    return {
      originator: 'DJ Kool Herc',
     technique: scratch.technique()
    };
  })
  .factory('scratch', function ($rootScope) {
    console.log('Called scratch!');
  return {
    technique: function () {
      return 'breakbeat';
    }
   };
  });
```

2. Now, take a look at this example spec that tests the service. Note that we have injected the `hiphop` module and assigned the injected `deejays` service to a variable so we can reference it within our tests. Finally, there is a single test with an expectation that the deejays service originator should match `DJ Kool Herc`:

```
describe('Service: deejays', function () {
  beforeEach(module('hiphop'));
    var deejays;
    beforeEach(inject(function ($injector) {
      deejays = $injector.get('deejays');
    }));
    it('should return the correct originator',function () {
    expect(deejays.originator).toBe('DJ Kool Herc');
  });
});
```

Running this spec with Jasmine will display the following results. Note that there is a log in the console window in the screenshot. This simply demonstrates that the scratch instance is actually run, giving us the console log. Therefore, the `deejays` factory has not been run in isolation.

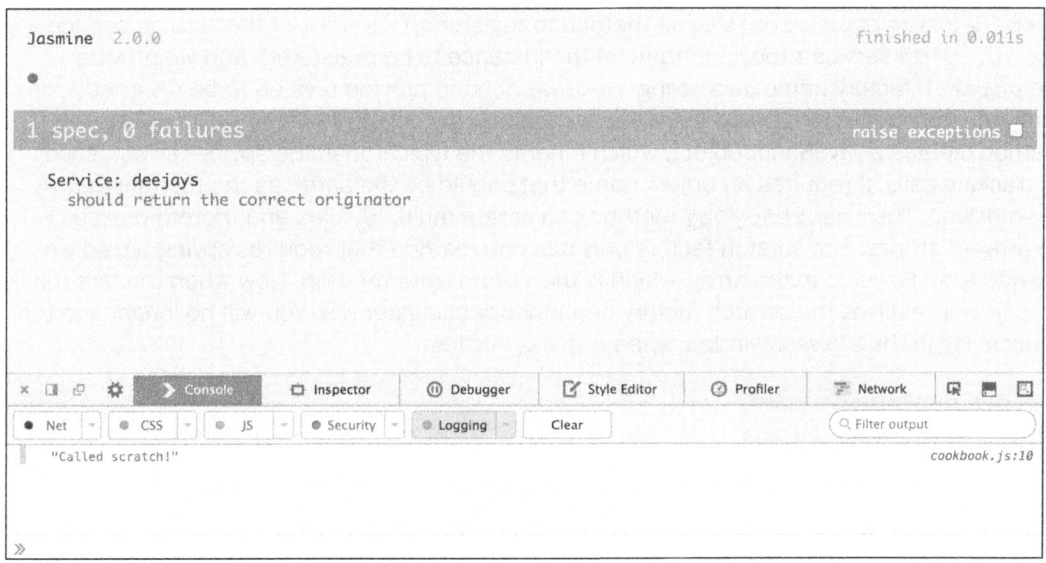

Both the `angular.js` and `angular-mocks.js` files are required to be included in your project and can be downloaded from `https://code.angularjs.org/1.2.28/`. Please refer to the *Running a simple test using Jasmine* recipe in *Chapter 1, Setup and Configuration*, to understand how these files are included in your code base.

How to do it...

Once you have understood the issue of module dependency through the examples on the sample module and spec, you are ready to start. Using the example spec from the *Getting ready* section of this recipe, perform the following steps:

1. First, below the `beforeEach()` method that loads the module, create a second `beforeEach()` method with the following code:

```
beforeEach(inject(function($provide) {
    $provide.value('scratch',
    jasmine.createSpyObj('scratch', ['technique']));
}));
```

2. If you now run the test again, you will notice that the console log no longer appears, indicating that the actual scratch module is not being used within the `deejay` test. This concludes the recipe!

How it works...

In step 1, we use the `$provide` service's (`https://docs.angularjs.org/api/auto/service/$provide`) `value` method to register an instance of the scratch service. The `$provide` service expects a name of the instance to be registered, and we provide the `scratch` factory name as a string. Next, we need to provide a value to be returned when the instance is requested, here we provide our spy object. Jasmine's `createSpyObj` method creates a JavaScript object, which inherits the typical Jasmine spy behaviour, such as tracking calls. It requires an object name that should be the same as the module that we are mocking. The `createSpyObj` method can create multiple spies and therefore expects an array of strings. The scratch factory only has one method that requires spying on, so we provide a single value in the array, which is the `technique` method. Now when the test runs, the injector resolves the scratch factory dependency using our spy. You will no longer see the console log in the browser window when running this test.

See also

▶ The *Mocking injected instances using an object* recipe in this chapter

▶ *Chapter 8, Service and Factory Testing with Mocks and Spies*

3
How to Test Navigation and Routing

In this chapter, you will learn the following recipes:

- ► Getting started with testing using ngRoute
- ► Testing route parameters with ngRoute
- ► Getting started with testing using ui-router
- ► Testing the transitioning state with ui-router
- ► Testing URL parameters with ui-router
- ► Testing page loading using Protractor
- ► Testing navigation using Protractor
- ► Testing redirection using Protractor

Introduction

AngularJS is a popular choice for developing **Single-Page Applications** (**SPA**), which have grown in popularity over the years. Navigating round an SPA, however, presents problems related to tracking location and state. AngularJS overcomes this dilemma by providing the ngRoute module (`https://docs.angularjs.org/api/ngRoute`) responsible for routing and deep linking services and directives. A popular alternative to ngRoute is the ui-router framework (`https://github.com/angular-ui/ui-router`). This chapter will guide you through testing some of the typical scenarios that you'll be presented with when using both ngRoute and ui-router. We will also make use of Protractor to run end-to-end tests, simulating user interaction for navigation.

To get started with the ngRoute module, include the text from `https://code.angularjs.org/1.2.28/angular-route.min.js` in the `angular-route.js` file within a script tag in your application and the `SpecRunner.html` file. Follow the same logic for ui-router using the the the script from `https://cdnjs.cloudflare.com/ajax/libs/angular-ui-router/0.2.10/angular-ui-router.js`.

Getting started with testing using ngRoute

To configure routes, we need to use the `$routeProvider` function; this maps paths from the current URL to a route object. The route object can include a controller, an HTML template, and other properties (for more information, visit `https://docs.angularjs.org/api/ngRoute/provider/$routeProvider`). This recipe will show you how to lay the initial groundwork to begin testing your routing logic, such as mapped values, and assigning route parameters to scope.

Getting ready

Ensure that you have included the `angular-route.js` file as documented in this chapter's introduction. You can use the following example code as a basis for testing in this recipe or use an existing application that includes ngRoute:

1. Load the ngRoute module in your application by adding it as a dependent module:

   ```
   angular.module('chapter3.ngRoute', ['ngRoute'])
   ```

2. Add a `config` block that will get applied during the application's bootstrap process. The `config` block injects providers, so this is where we supply a `$routeProvider` function to configure our routes. For this example, we simply define a single route named `/home` that requires a reference to the controller defined in the following code as `HomeCtrl`, and provides a simple header as the template:

```
angular.module('chapter3.ngRoute', ['ngRoute'])
  .config(['$routeProvider', function($routeProvider) {
      $routeProvider
          .when('/emcees/:id', {
              controller: 'EmceesCtrl'
          })
          .when('/home', {
              templateUrl: 'home.html',
              controller: 'HomeCtrl'
          })
          .otherwise({
              redirectTo: '/'
          });
```

For further information on configuration of ngRoute, please refer to the documentation at `https://docs.angularjs.org/api/ngRoute`. Also, ensure that you've loaded your module as shown in the following code:

```
beforeEach(module('chapter3.ngRoute'));
```

How to do it...

1. First, let's create a basic test to ensure that the correct controller is mapped to the specified route and inject the dependencies required for this test:

```
it('route controller should be mapped to HomeCtrl',
inject(function ($rootScope, $location, $route) {}));
```

2. Next, within the test from step 1, use the `$location` service and set the path to `/home`:

```
$location.path('/home');
```

3. After setting the path, add `rootScope.$apply()` to ensure that changes are propagated:

```
rootScope.$apply();
```

4. Finally, add the expectation that the route current controller path is equal to the expected value:

```
expect($route.current.controller).toEqual('HomeCtrl');
```

5. The final code should look as follows:

```
it('route controller should be mapped to HomeCtrl',
inject(function($rootScope, $location, $route) {
    $location.path('/home');
    $rootScope.$apply();
    expect($route.current.controller).toEqual('HomeCtrl');
}));
```

How it works...

To summarize what we are testing in this recipe, we have configured our router to use our specified controller when navigating to a particular location. Within our test, we need to navigate to the specific location and ensure that the current route definition returns the correct controller.

In step 1, we define our test intention and inject the required dependencies. The $location service replaces the dependency on global objects, such as a window, which makes testing difficult. The $location path() method is a *getter* or a *setter* that returns or sets the path of the current URL. In step 2, we use the $location path method (https://docs. angularjs.org/api/ng/service/$location) to set the current path to /home.

In step 4, we use the current property on the $route provider to access the controller constructor as defined in the route definition. The returned value is then used in a toEqual matcher to compare against our expected string of HomeCtrl.

There's more...

As we saw earlier, the current property on the $route provider allows us which makes the current route definition. Quite often, supplying a simple template is not enough and you, therefore, may replace the template property with templateUrl and it should return a path to an HTML template.

If your configured routes are expected to load templates using templateUrl, then they will have to be satisfied as a dependency. The easiest way to do this is to cache a template using the $templateCache service (https://docs.angularjs.org/api/ng/service/$templateCache) and while using this approach, the template HTML file need not even exist. For example, you can add the following code to a beforeEach function ensuring that the template is cached prior to each test:

```
$templateCache.put('home.html', 'Some template content');
```

You can then write a test once again using the current property on the $route provider accessing the current route definition of the templateUrl funtion:

```
it('route templateUrl should be home.html', inject(function
($rootScope, $location, $route) {
  $location.path('/home');
  $rootScope.$apply();
  expect($route.current.templateUrl).toEqual('home.html');
}));
```

See also

► The *Testing route parameters with ngRoute* recipe in this chapter

Testing route parameters with ngRoute

Route parameters are used to pass additional data to the URL, for example, ID or key-value pairs. This additional data may be used as query parameters or for RESTful routing (http://rest.elkstein.org/). This recipe will guide you on testing route parameters with the $routeParams service (https://docs.angularjs.org/api/ngRoute/service/$routeParams).

Getting ready

To get started, you'll need to define a route with parameters, either within an existing application or using the example code given here. In this example, the emcees name could be a page listing various emcee names and then a path with an id would show a page of a specific emcee based on the provided id value. To test the parameters, we access and assign the route parameters to scope in a controller:

1. First, load the ngRoute module in your application by adding it as a dependent module:

   ```
   angular.module('chapter3.ngRoute', ['ngRoute'])
   ```

2. Next, add a config block that will get applied during the application's bootstrap process. Supply a $routeProvider function to the config block. Add a route definition using the when() method (https://docs.angularjs.org/api/ngRoute/provider/$routeProvider#when) with a path to the route named emcees. Append a named group to the path starting with a colon and call it id. The group named id will be replaced with a provided routeParam service of the same name (https://docs.angularjs.org/api/ngRoute/service/$routeParams). Finally, provide a route object mapping to a controller named EmceesCtrl:

```
angular.module('chapter3.ngRoute', ['ngRoute'])
    .config(['$routeProvider', function($routeProvider) {
        $routeProvider
            .when('/emcees/:id', {
                controller: 'EmceesCtrl'
            })
            .when('/home', {
                templateUrl: 'home.html',
                controller: 'HomeCtrl'
            })
            .otherwise({
                redirectTo: '/'
            });
    }])
```

3. Finally, create a controller associated with the route from step 2 that accesses the injected `$routeParams` service and assigns the value of `id` to scope:

```
.controller('EmceesCtrl', ['$scope', '$routeParams',
function($scope, $routeParams) {
  $scope.id = $routeParams.id;
}]);
```

4. Also, ensure that you've loaded your module, for example:

```
beforeEach(module('chapter3.ngRoute'));
```

How to do it...

To test route parameters, we will need a defined route that passes this logic. We simply need to mock the `$routeParams` service, which is as easy as adding an additional object to the controller configuration:

1. First, let's create a basic test checking the route parameters and inject the dependencies required for this test:

```
it('should assign routeParams to scope', inject(function
($rootScope, $controller) {}));
```

2. Next, create a new scope object:

```
var scope = $rootScope.$new();
```

3. Register a new instance of our controller providing the scope object created in step 2 and a `$routeParams` object with an `id` value:

```
$controller('EmceesCtrl', {
  $scope: scope,
  $routeParams: {
    id: '1'
  }
});
```

4. Finally, add the expectation that the scope `id` has the same value we provided to the `$routeParams` object:

```
expect(scope.id).toEqual('1');
```

How it works...

It is quite easy to overcomplicate testing, and routing can be a classic example of this. The $routeParams service simply allows you to retrieve the current set of route parameters. In step 3, to gain complete control of what is being assigned to the $routeParams service, we simply create an object and inject it into the controller maintaining test isolation. We expect that the controller then assigns the $routeParams object ID value to scope and we test this in step 4.

See also

► The *Getting started with testing using ngRoute* recipe in this chapter

Getting started with testing using ui-router

The ui-router framework is similar to ngRoute but more powerful due to easy implementation of nested states and views, named views, and so on. Although the $stateProvider ui-router is similar to $routeProvider, its emphasis on state allows an impressive management of the application's interface.

In this recipe, we will we will test states within an AngularJS application using the ui-router framework.

Getting ready

This recipe requires a project that utilizes the ui-router framework and is configured using $stateProvider with at least one state. At the start of this chapter, I gave some example code that demonstrates configuring $stateProvider with a state called home and also assigns a templateUrl function and a controller to the state. If you're unfamiliar with ui-router, I suggest that you take advantage of the example code. Testing is also a great way to start understanding libraries and frameworks:

1. First, load the ui.router module in your application by adding it as a dependent module:

```
angular.module('chapter3.ui.router', ['ui.router'])
```

2. Next, add a `config` block that will get applied during the application's bootstrap process:

```
angular.module('chapter3.ui.router', ['ui.router'])
  .config(['$urlRouterProvider', '$stateProvider',
  function($urlRouterProvider, $stateProvider) {
    $stateProvider
    .state('home', {
      url: '/home',
      templateUrl: 'home.html'
    })
    $urlRouterProvider
    .otherwise('/home');
  }]);
```

The preceding code can be broken down and explained in the following steps:

1. Supply a `$stateProvider` service to the `config` block.

2. Add a state (`https://github.com/angular-ui/ui-router/wiki`) named home with a `config` object.

3. Set the URL property and a value of `/home`. This is associated with the state (`https://github.com/angular-ui/ui-router/wiki/URL-Routing`).

4. Set the `templateUrl` property and a `home.html` value.

5. Supply a `$urlRouterProvider` service to the `config` block (`https://github.com/angular-ui/ui-router/wiki/URL-Routing#urlrouterprovider`) that watches the `$location` service. Using the `otherwise()` method (`https://github.com/angular-ui/ui-router/wiki/URL-Routing#otherwise-for-invalid-routes`), we ensure that the locations that have not been configured are redirected to `/home`.

6. Also, ensure that you've loaded your module, for example:

```
beforeEach(module('chapter3.ui.router'));
```

How to do it...

1. First, cache our template within a `beforeEach()` method to ensure that it's loaded prior to all tests:

```
beforeEach(inject(function($templateCache) {
  $templateCache.put('home.html', '');
}));
```

2. Next, create a test detailing our intention and inject the required dependencies:

```
it('default state should be home', inject(function
($rootScope, $state) {}));
```

3. Simulate the scope life cycle using the following:

```
$rootScope.$apply();
```

4. Finally, add the expectation that the state's current name property has a home value:

```
expect($state.current.name).toEqual('home');
```

How it works...

As we configured `ui.router` with a `templateUrl` function, in step 1 we need to follow the logic documented in the *Getting started with testing using ngRoute* recipe in this chapter, and cache our template.

We don't need to define a location or state in our test, as we have defined a redirection to the home state using `$urlRouterProvider` (refer to the *Getting started* section for this recipe). This makes our testing a whole lot easier. We simulate the scope life cycle in step 3, and then in step 4 we use `$state service` (http://angular-ui.github.io/ui-router/site/#/api/ui.router.state.$state) to access the current state object name property. Our expectation is that the current state name should equal home.

There's more...

Using the `$state` service current state object, we can also test whether the current state `templateUrl` is as expected:

```
it('state templateUrl should be home.html',
inject(function($rootScope, $state) {
  $rootScope.$apply();
  expect($state.current.templateUrl).toEqual('home.html');
}));
```

Additionally, we can test that the controller is as we expect:

```
it('state controller should be HomeCtrl',
inject(function($rootScope, $state) {
  $rootScope.$apply();
  expect($state.current.controller).toEqual('HomeCtrl');
}));
```

See also

- ▸ The *Testing the transitioning state with ui-router* recipe
- ▸ The *Testing URL parameters with ui-router* recipe

Testing the transitioning state with ui-router

The `$stateProvider` ui-router focuses purely on state (`https://github.com/angular-ui/ui-router/wiki`). Some examples of how you can update the state within your application are responding to user interaction or specific data change events. The ui-router makes it incredibly easy to transition state, and in this recipe, we will demonstrate how to test this.

Getting ready

Follow the *Getting ready* section in the *Getting started with testing using ui-router* recipe in this chapter, to set up with the ui-router basics. We don't necessarily need the `templateUrl` function, so that can be removed. In addition to this, add a second state that we can transition to the named `emcees` objects:

```
.state('emcees', {
  url: '/emcees'
});
```

Also, ensure that you've loaded your module, for example:

```
beforeEach(module('chapter3.ui.router'));
```

How to do it...

1. First, create some local variables that can be accessed across all the tests in this recipe:

   ```
   var scope;
   var state;
   ```

2. Next, inject the required dependencies and assign the relevant values to the variables created in step 1 within a `beforeEach()` function:

   ```
   beforeEach(inject(function($rootScope, $state) {
     scope = $rootScope.$new();
     state = $state;
   }));
   ```

3. Now, write a simple test to ensure that the default current state is as expected:

```
it('default state should be home', function () {
  scope.$apply();
  expect(state.current.name).toEqual('home');
});
```

4. Based on the previous step demonstrating our default current state, we can now test transitioning to a different state. Create the following additional test and transition to the emcees state using the go() method:

```
it('should transition to emcees state', function () {
  state.go('emcees');
  scope.$apply();
});
```

5. Finally, add the expectation to test whether the current state name matches the state we aimed to transition to:

```
expect(state.current.name).toEqual('emcees');
```

6. You should see the following passing test within your browser (refer to the *Running a simple test using Jasmine* recipe in *Chapter 1, Setup and Configuration*, if you've forgotten how to produce this output):

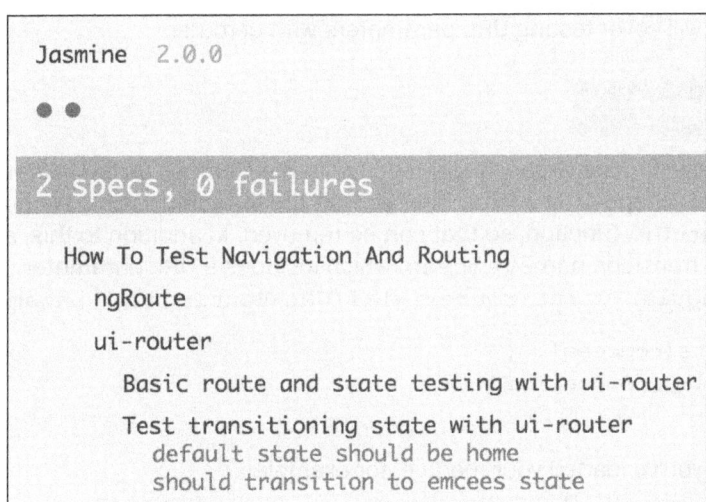

How it works...

In step 3, we use the `$state` service's current state object name property and determine that it matches our default current state. In step 4, using the state `go()` method (`https://github.com/angular-ui/ui-router/wiki/Quick-Reference#stategoto--toparams--options`), we triggered a transition to the `emcees` state. In step 7, once again, we check the `$state` service's current state object name property and expect it to equal our `emcees` state that we transitioned to.

See also

 ▶   The *Getting started with testing using ui-router* recipe in this chapter
 ▶   The *Testing URL parameters with ui-router* recipe in this chapter

Testing URL parameters with ui-router

URLs can pass additional information that ui-router can then access using the `$stateParams` service (`https://github.com/angular-ui/ui-router/wiki/URL-Routing#stateparams-service`). The `$stateParams` service is an object matching individual parts of the navigated URL and provides these parts to controllers and services. In this recipe, we will cover testing URL parameters with ui-router.

Getting ready

Follow the steps given in the *Getting ready* section in the *Getting started with testing using ui-router* recipe in this chapter to become familiar with the ui-router basics. We don't necessarily need the `templateUrl` function, so that can be removed. In addition to this, add a second state that we can transition named `emcees`, which includes a URL parameter (`https://github.com/angular-ui/ui-router/wiki/URL-Routing#url-parameters`):

```
.state('emcees', {
  url: '/emcees/:id'
});
```

Also, ensure that you've loaded your module, for example:

```
beforeEach(module('chapter3.ui.router'));
```

How to do it...

1. First, create some local variables to access across all the tests in this recipe:

```
var scope;
var state;
```

2. Next, inject the required dependencies and assign the relevant values to the variables created in step 1 within a `beforeEach()` function:

```
beforeEach(inject(function($rootScope, $state) {
  scope = $rootScope.$new();
  state = $state;
}));
```

3. Next, write a simple test to confirm the parameters:

```
it('should transition to emcees state passing the correct id
param', function() {
  state.go('emcees', {id:'1'});
  scope.$apply();
    });
```

4. Finally, add the expectation that the state `params` object contains the same `id` provided when triggering the state transition:

```
expect(state.params.id).toEqual(id);
```

How it works...

In step 3, using the state `go()` method, we triggered a transition to the `emcees` state providing an object with an `id` property as an additional parameter. In step 4, we checked the `$state` service `params` object `id` property and expected it to equal our `emcees` state that we transitioned to.

See also

▶ The *Getting started with testing using ui-router* recipe
▶ The *Testing the transitioning state with ui-router* recipe

Testing page loading using Protractor

This recipe will guide you through an end-to-end test with Protractor. This test will simply ensure that our routing logic works by confirming that the URL in the browser matches our expectation. Protractor enables us to replicate user interaction within an actual browser offering additional assurance that the code logic works as expected.

Getting ready

For this recipe, we can build on the steps from the *Getting ready* section from the *Testing URL parameters with ui-router* recipe in this chapter. This will provide us with a default `home` state and the `emcees` state to transition to. We don't necessarily need the `templateUrl` function, so that can be removed. Follow the following steps to create an example for this recipe:

1. Add a state to the HTML as per the ui-router documentation (`https://github.com/angular-ui/ui-router/wiki#the-simplest-form-of-state`):

   ```
   <div ui-view></div>
   ```

2. Also ensure that you've loaded your module, for example:

   ```
   beforeEach(module('chapter3.ui.router'));
   ```

   For further information on running Protractor, please read the *Installing Protractor* recipe in *Chapter 1, Setup and Configuration*.

How to do it...

1. Firstly, we need to ensure that Protractor navigates our browser to the correct URL, that is, our local server and port:

   ```
   beforeEach(function () {
     browser.get('http://0.0.0.0:8000/');
   });
   ```

2. Next, create a test stating our intention:

   ```
   it('should default to home page', function () {});
   ```

3. Finally, add an expectation to match the browser's location against our expected value:

   ```
   expect(browser.getLocationAbsUrl()).toContain('/home');
   ```

4. You will see the following result in your console:

```
paranoia:chapter_3 newtriks$ protractor protractor.conf.js
Using the selenium server at http://localhost:4444/wd/hub
.

Finished in 2.712 seconds
1 test, 1 assertion, 0 failures
```

How it works...

Protractor offers a global variable named `browser` that is used for browser-level commands and is a wrapper around the instance of WebDriver. Please visit `https://github.com/angular/protractor/blob/master/docs/api-overview.md#global-variables` for further global variables available. With the AngularJS library available, we are able to use the `get` method in step 1 to load our application by passing the URL to the local development server running our application. We expect the router to ensure that the correct default page has loaded at this point.

In step 3, we again use a browser-level command named `getLocationAbsUrl` to access the absolute URL. Finally using the `toContain` matcher, we can confirm that our expected state URL is within the returned full path.

There's more...

To test whether there is a specific element you expect on the page, you can use Protractor locators. Using the global function named element, we can use a locator and expect it to return `ElementFinder` (`https://github.com/angular/protractor/blob/master/docs/api.md#elementfinder`). An `ElementFinder` feature enables us to call actions on the element, for example `click()`. In this example, we use the `buttonText` locator to locate the button with a label load. We then confirm that the element is present on the page as expected, using the `isPresent` function:

```
it('should show a load button on home page', function () {
  var button = element(by.buttonText('load'));
  expect(button.isPresent()).toBeTruthy();
});
```

See also

▶ The *Testing navigation using Protractor* recipe
▶ The *Installing Protractor* recipe in *Chapter 1, Setup and Configuration*

Testing navigation using Protractor

When testing navigation, it would be great to actually load and navigate through states within a browser. Luckily, we can do just that using Protractor. This is quite compelling, because, typically, to test interactive route changes we would expect a manual process whereby a user would have to load the page in a browser and interact with elements, for example clicking a button to trigger a route/state change. We can configure Protractor to follow a defined set of instructions and mimic user actions thereby saving a lot of our time and effort plus enabling a greater spectrum of application testing. In this recipe, we will test navigation through an AngularJS application based on element interaction using Protractor.

Getting ready

For this recipe, we can build on the steps from the *Getting ready* section from the *Testing URL parameters with ui-router* recipe in this chapter. This will provide us with a default home state and the `emcees` state to transition to. We don't necessarily need the `templateUrl` function so that can be removed. In addition to this setup, we add a button and click handler that will transition the state. A value will be passed through to the handler and will be provided as a URL parameter:

1. Add a state to the HTML as per the ui-router documentation (`https://github.com/angular-ui/ui-router/wiki#the-simplest-form-of-state`) and a button that makes use of `ng-click` to call a handler method:

   ```
   <div ui-view>
     <button ng-click="loadEmcee(1)">load</button>
   </div>
   ```

2. Add a controller with the handler method that transitions state with a defined parameter:

   ```
   .controller('HomeCtrl', ['$scope', '$state', function($scope,
   $state) {
     $scope.loadEmcee = function(id) {
       $state.go('emcees', {
         id: id
       });
     }
   }])
   ```

3. Also, ensure that you've loaded your module, for example:

   ```
   beforeEach(module('chapter3.ui.router'));
   ```

   For further information on running Protractor, please read the *Installing Protractor* recipe in *Chapter 1, Setup and Configuration*.

How to do it...

1. Firstly, use the `get` method to load the page by passing the URL to the local development server running our application:

```
beforeEach(function () {
  browser.get('http://0.0.0.0:8000/');
});
```

2. Next, create a test stating our intention:

```
it(should navigate to emcees page on click of the load
button', function () {});
```

3. Using the `buttonText` locator, locate the button with a label `load`:

```
var button = element(by.buttonText('load'));
```

4. Next, use the click action on the element:

```
button.click();
```

5. Finally, add an expectation to match the browser's location against our expected value:

```
expect(browser.getLocationAbsUrl()).toContain('/emcees');
```

How it works...

In step 3, we use the `ElementFinder` reference to find the button element based on its label. In step 4, we call a click action that triggers the click event on the button within the DOM. We have configured a click handler in our application code that will navigate to the emcees state. The `getLocationAbsUrl` function returns the full URL and we use the `toContain` matcher to confirm that our expected state URL of `emcees` is within the returned full path.

There's more...

To test URL parameters using Protractor, we can simply update the matcher to include the expected URL parameter, for example:

```
expect(browser.getLocationAbsUrl()).toContain('/emcees/1');
```

As your end-to-end test suites grow, you may want to consider encapsulating information about the elements on your application page using Page Objects (`http://angular.github.io/protractor/#/page-objects`). This can also help with code reuse across multiple tests.

See also

- The *Testing page loading using Protractor* recipe in this chapter
- The *Installing Protractor* recipe in *Chapter 1, Setup and Configuration*
- The *Testing navigation using Protractor* recipe in this chapter

Testing redirection using Protractor

What if a user enters a URL that has not been registered with $stateProvider? We may expect the application to fallback to a specific state. Using ui-router, you can use the otherwise method on the $urlRouterProvider service to define the state to fallback to. In this recipe, we will learn how to test whether an application redirects to a specified state if the URL entered has not been registered with $stateProvider.

Getting ready

For this recipe, we can use the minimal setup to provide us with a default home state. We then use the $urlRouterProvider otherwise() method to handle redirecting an invalid route (https://github.com/angular-ui/ui-router/wiki/URL-Routing#otherwise-for-invalid-routes):

1. Add a state to the HTML as per the ui-router documentation at https://github.com/angular-ui/ui-router/wiki#the-simplest-form-of-state:

   ```
   <div ui-view></div>
   ```

2. Add the following configuration block with a single $state function called /home and use the $urlRouterProvider otherwise() method to redirect to this state when there is an invalid route provided. Please refer to the *Getting started with testing using ui-router* recipe in this chapter for further information:

   ```
   .config(['$urlRouterProvider', '$stateProvider',
   function($urlRouterProvider, $stateProvider) {
       $stateProvider
         .state('home', {
           url: '/home',
           templateUrl: 'home.html',
           controller: 'HomeCtrl'
         })
         .state('emcees', {
           url: '/emcees/:id'
         });
       $urlRouterProvider
         .otherwise('/home');
   }])
   ```

3. Also, ensure that you've loaded your module, for example:

```
beforeEach(module('chapter3.ui.router'));
```

For further information on running Protractor, please read the *Installing Protractor* recipe in *Chapter 1, Setup and Configuration*.

How to do it...

1. Firstly, create a test stating our intention:

```
it(should navigate to emcees page on click of the load
button', function () {});
```

2. To test the fallback, simply use the `get` method to load an unknown URL:

```
browser.get('http://0.0.0.0:8000/#/dummy');
```

3. Finally, simply match the browser URL against the expected fallback:

```
expect(browser.getLocationAbsUrl()).toContain('/home);
```

4. The final test function should look as follows:

```
it('should redirect to home page if an unknown url is provided',
function () {
    browser.get('http://0.0.0.0:8000/#/dummy');
    expect(browser.getLocationAbsUrl()).toContain('/home');
});
```

How it works...

In step 2, we use the `get` method to load a URL that has not been registered with `$stateProvider` and expect our application to fallback to the state defined in the `otherwise` method on the `$urlRouterProvider` service. Step 3 uses the `getLocationAbsUrl` function that returns the full URL and we use the `toContain` matcher to confirm that our expected state URL of `/home` is within the returned full path.

See also

▶ The *Testing navigation using Protractor* recipe

▶ The *Testing page loading using Protractor* recipe

▶ The *Installing Protractor* recipe in *Chapter 1, Setup and Configuration*

4

Testing Controllers

In this chapter, you will learn the following recipes:

- ▸ Setting up for testing a controller
- ▸ Testing the initial state of a scope object
- ▸ Testing the initial state of a scope object with Protractor
- ▸ Testing interactive scope changes with Protractor
- ▸ Testing navigation scope changes with Protractor

Introduction

Business logic for a single view can be found in a controller. Controllers are used for configuring the initial `$scope` object or adding behavior to `$scope`. DOM manipulation, however, should not be managed within controllers. For further information regarding AngularJS controllers, please read the online documentation at `https://docs.angularjs.org/guide/controller`. Considering what we've just discussed, tests should be focused either on modifications to the scope object or its associated behavior. A scope can be an assigned initial property that provides the view with data. These properties are then updated either via user interaction or from external services. Scope behavior is constructed by attaching methods to the scope object. This chapter will focus on how to set up a test for testing a controller and pay particular attention to the tasks we would expect to be handled within a controller.

Setting up for testing a controller

The set up for testing a controller is simple, and this recipe will ensure that you have a solid foundation ready to build on as you progress through this chapter.

Getting ready

To begin with this recipe, you'll simply need a project setup with a controller. In this recipe for example, we use a controller named `SomeCtrl`; make sure you replace this with the name of the controller you're testing.

How to do it...

1. First, create two variables accessible across all tests:
   - One for the root scope: `var rootScope;`
   - One for scope: `var scope;`

2. Ensure that you load your module:
   ```
   beforeEach(module('chapter4'));
   ```

3. Create a `beforeEach` function to inject the necessary dependencies and assign them to the variables declared in step 1:
   ```
   beforeEach(inject(function ($rootScope) {
     rootScope = $rootScope;
     scope = $rootScope.$new();
   }));
   ```

4. Finally, create another `beforeEach` function to inject the `$controller` service to register a new instance of our controller providing the scope object created in step 2:
   ```
   beforeEach(inject(function ($controller) {
     $controller('SomeCtrl', {
       $scope: scope
     });
   }));
   ```

How it works...

Step 4 is the key step in setting up testing controllers and relies on the injected `$controller` service. The injected `$controller` service enables us to register a new instance of our controller with the injector. The `$controller` service is passed a string that's used to retrieve the controller constructor. The second argument that we provide is an object that is used to inject locals into the controller. This is the location where you can inject mock and spy data or services to thoroughly test your controllers.

The object key must match the variable name of the injected resource it's replacing.

We provide the scope object created in step 3 to be injected into the newly created controller instance, which enables us to match expectations on scope values throughout tests.

See also

▶ The *Testing the initial state of a scope object* recipe

Testing the initial state of a scope object

Scope properties are used in controllers and attached to the DOM. These properties are then accessed through bindings within a view. Typically, an initial state is defined on scope properties. This recipe will guide you through testing a scope property to see whether it has the expected initialized state.

Getting ready

Ensure that you have a project set up with a controller. In this recipe, we have a controller named SomeCtrl; please replace this with the name of the controller you're testing. Also ensure that you have a scope property to test against. Here is the example code to create a new module and a simple controller that assigns a value of foo to scope:

```
angular.module('chapter4', []);
var SomeCtrl = function ($scope) {
  $scope.id = 'foo';
};
```

Finally, attach scope to the view using the ngController directive:

```
<div ng-controller="SomeCtrl">
  {{id}}
</div>
```

How to do it...

1. Create a `beforeEach` function to inject the necessary dependencies and assign them to global variables:

```
beforeEach(inject(function ($rootScope) {
  scope = $rootScope.$new();
}));
```

2. Next, create another `beforeEach` function to inject the `$controller` service to register a new instance of our controller providing the scope object created in step 1:

```
beforeEach(inject(function ($controller) {
  $controller('SomeCtrl', {
    $scope: scope
  });
}));
```

3. Create a basic test to establish that the initial scope property value is what we expect:

```
it('should set the scope property id to the correct initial
value', function () {});
```

4. Finally, add the expectation that the `id` scope property matches `foo`:

```
expect(scope.id).toBe('foo');
```

5. You should see the following passing test within your browser:

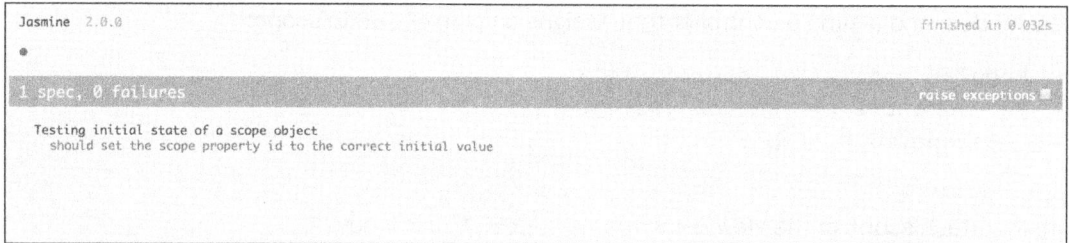

How it works...

In step 2, when the new instance of the controller is registered, we provide the scope object that we had previously assigned to a global variable in step 1. This enables us to access the scope object throughout our tests and as it is updated within the controller and determine whether the initial value was as expected as shown in step 4.

See also

▶ The *Setting up for testing a controller* recipe

Testing the initial state of a scope object with Protractor

We can use the power of Protractor to confirm the scope data model from the view's perspective, which initializes with the default parameter we define. This recipe will show you how to use Protractor to load the initial state in a browser and target the bound view element to determine its value.

Getting ready

For this recipe, you will need to have a scope property defined and rendered in a view. Ensure you have Protractor installed and running and if you need guidance on setting up Protractor please read the *Installing Protractor* recipe in *Chapter 1, Setup and Configuration*. Please update your URL and port based on your configuration. Additionally, here is an example of a Protractor configuration used in this recipe for testing:

```
exports.config = {
  seleniumAddress: 'http://localhost:4444/wd/hub',
  specs: ['test/cookbookSpec.e2e.js'],
  jasmineNodeOpts: {
    showColors: true,
    defaultTimeoutInterval: 30000
  }
};
```

How to do it...

1. Firstly, we need to ensure that Protractor navigates our browser to the correct URL, that is, our local server and port:

    ```
    beforeEach(function () {
      browser.get('http://0.0.0.0:8000/');
    });
    ```

2. Next, create a base test to ensure that the default initialized value of the id scope property id is what we would expect:

    ```
    it('should initialize scope parameter id to expected
    value', function () {});
    ```

3. Now, let's add a reference to the element with the binding of id to this test:

    ```
    var el = element(by.binding('id'));
    ```

4. Add an expectation that the element text matches the scope property value:

    ```
    expect(el.getText()).toEqual('foo');
    ```

5. If you run Protractor now, you should see the following result in your console:

```
paranoia:chapter_4 newtriks$ protractor protractor.conf.js
Using the selenium server at http://localhost:4444/wd/hub

.

Finished in 2.982 seconds
1 test, 1 assertion, 0 failures
```

How it works...

Using the binding Protractor locator in step 3, we find the element in the DOM that is bound to the `id` property on the scope. Once we have a reference to the element, we can ascertain its text value using the `getText` action, as seen in step 4.

See also

▸ The *Testing navigation scope changes with Protractor* recipe

▸ The *Installing Protractor* recipe in *Chapter 1, Setup and Configuration*

Testing interactive scope changes with Protractor

More often than not, we would expect a scope data model to be updated based on user interaction with the view (through AngularJS data binding). This recipe will guide you through replicating user actions with Protractor and testing view model updates based on these actions.

Getting ready

For this recipe, you will need to have a scope property defined and rendered in a view. You will also need to have the necessary logic to update the data model via a user-defined action. For example, here is the code that configures a scope property named `id` that's defined in a view template. Then, there's a button that registers a click event with a scope method called `update`:

```
<body ng-controller="SomeCtrl">
  <div>
    {{id}}
  </div>
  <button class="btn" ng-click="update()">Update</button>
</body>
```

When the update method is called, we simply change the `id` property on the scope and expect this to be propagated through to the view.

```
var SomeCtrl = function($scope) {
  $scope.id = 'foo';
  $scope.update = function() {
    $scope.id = 'bar';
  }
};
```

Ensure that you have Protractor installed and running and if you need guidance on setting up Protractor, please read the *Installing Protractor* recipe in *Chapter 1, Setup and Configuration*. Please update your URL and port based on your configuration.

How to do it...

1. Firstly, we need to ensure that Protractor navigates our browser to the correct URL, that is, to our local server and port:

    ```
    beforeEach(function () {
      browser.get('http://0.0.0.0:8000/');
    });
    ```

2. Create a test stating our intention:

    ```
    it('should update scope parameter id to expected value',
    function () {});
    ```

3. Using the abbreviated version of the locator for CSS selectors, call the `click` action:

    ```
    $('.btn').click();
    ```

4. Add a reference to the element with the binding of `id`:

    ```
    var el = element(by.binding('id'));
    ```

5. Finally, add an expectation that the element text matches the updated scope property value:

    ```
    expect(el.getText()).toEqual('bar');
    ```

6. Now if you run protractor, then you should see that there has been a test run with one assertion and no failures.

How it works...

In step 3, we use a Protractor locator that finds an element using a CSS selector (we used the shortcut $() notation). Using the click action that (you guessed it) clicks the element, we would then expect the sequence of events such as, to update scope, and the view, to take place. In step 4, we find the element in the DOM that is bound to the id property on the scope, and then in step 5 we use the getText action to retrieve the text value to evaluate against the test matcher.

See also

▶ The *Testing the initial state of a scope object with Protractor* recipe

▶ The *Testing navigation scope changes with Protractor* recipe

▶ The *Installing Protractor* recipe in *Chapter 1, Setup and Configuration*

Testing navigation scope changes with Protractor

As demonstrated in the previous recipe, *Testing interactive scope changes with Protractor*, data models are modified on user interaction with the view. Obviously, there are other mechanisms to modify scope properties, one of which is navigation. This recipe will guide you through testing a controller that makes changes to scope properties upon navigation. For this recipe, we will use the ui-router (https://github.com/angular-ui/ui-router) for application routing and, basically, navigate between two states updating a scope property based on a state parameter passed during routing.

Getting ready

For this recipe, you will need to have a scope property defined and rendered in a view. You will also need to have the necessary logic to update the data model on navigation, whether using a ui-router or another routing option. For the recipe example, here are the steps to follow:

1. Define a handler in a controller to navigate the state using the provided value, id:

```
var HomeCtrl = function($scope, $state) {
  $scope.id = 'foo';
  $scope.loadEmcee = function(id) {
    $state.go('emcees', {
      id: id
    });
  }
};
```

2. Next, create a second controller that is initialized when its defined state is loaded. In this instance, the controller uses the injected state parameters to assign the `id` value to `$scope.id`:

```
var EmceeCtrl = function($scope, $stateParams) {
  $scope.id = $stateParams.id;
};
```

3. Next, add the HTML code to navigate the state using a button click event, passing in a value to be used as a state parameter:

```
<body ng-controller="HomeCtrl">
  <div ui-view>
    {{id}}
  </div>
  <button class="btn" ng-click="loadEmcee(1)">Emcee 1</button>
</body>
```

4. Finally, the router is configured with two states, as follows:

```
var UIRouterConfig = function($urlRouterProvider,
$stateProvider) {
  $stateProvider
    .state('home', {
      url: '/home',
      controller: 'HomeCtrl'
    })
    .state('emcees', {
      url: '/emcees/:id',
      controller: 'EmceeCtrl'
    });
  $urlRouterProvider
  .otherwise('/home');
};
```

Ensure that you have Protractor installed and running, and if you need guidance on setting up Protractor, please read the *Installing Protractor* recipe in *Chapter 1*, *Setup and Configuration*. Also update your URL and port based on your configuration.

How to do it...

1. Firstly, we need to ensure that Protractor navigates our browser to the correct URL that is, to our local server and port:

```
beforeEach(function () {
  browser.get('http://0.0.0.0:8000/');
});
```

2. Next, create a test stating our intention:

```
it(should update scope parameter id to expected value on
navigation', function () {});
```

3. Using the locator for CSS selectors, call the `click` action on the returned element:

```
$('.btn').click();
```

4. Next, add a reference to the element with the binding of `id`:

```
var el = element(by.binding('id'));
```

5. Finally, add an expectation such that the element text matches the updated scope property value following the navigation:

```
expect(el.getText()).toEqual('1');
```

6. If you now run Protractor, then you should see that there has been a test run with one assertion and no failures.

How it works...

The sequence of events is similar to the *Testing interactive scope changes with Protractor* recipe in this chapter. The `click` action in step 3 triggers the button in the DOM to dispatch the `click` event passing a value of 1, in this example. If the state navigation works as we expect, then `EmceeCtrl` will assign the `$stateParams` id property to the `$scope` id property. We confirm this in step 5 using the `getText` action to retrieve the text value for the matcher.

See also

▶ The *Testing the initial state of a scope object with Protractor* recipe

▶ The *Testing interactive scope changes with Protractor* recipe

▶ The *Installing Protractor* recipe in *Chapter 1, Setup and Configuration*

▶ The *Testing navigation using Protractor* recipe in *Chapter 3, How To Test Navigation and Routing*

5
Testing User Interaction and Directives

In this chapter, we will cover the following recipes:

- ► Starting with testing directives
- ► Setting up templateUrl
- ► Searching elements using selectors
- ► Accessing basic HTML content
- ► Accessing repeater content
- ► Scope changes based on user input
- ► Scope changes based on DOM events
- ► Class changes based on window properties
- ► Directive changes on interaction using Protractor

Introduction

Directives are the cornerstone of AngularJS and can range in complexity providing the foundation to many aspects of an application. Therefore, directives require comprehensive tests to ensure they are interacting with the DOM as intended. This chapter will guide you through some of the rudimentary steps required to embark on your journey to test directives. The focal point of many of the recipes revolves around targeting specific HTML elements and how they respond to interaction. You will learn how to test changes on scope based on a range of influences and finally begin addressing testing directives using Protractor.

Starting with testing directives

Testing a directive involves three key steps that we will address in this recipe to serve as a foundation for the duration of this chapter:

1. Create an element.

2. Compile the element and link to a scope object.

3. Simulate the scope life cycle.

Getting ready

For this recipe, you simply need a directive that applies a scope value to the element in the DOM. For example:

```
angular.module('chapter5', [])
  .directive('writers', function() {
    return {
      restrict: 'E',
      link: function(scope, element) {
        element.text('Graffiti artist: ' + scope.artist);
      }
    };
  });
```

How to do it...

1. First, create three variables accessible across all tests:

    - One for the element: `var element;`

    - One for scope: `var scope;`

    - One for some dummy data to assign to a scope value: `var artist = 'Amara Por Dios';`

2. Next, ensure that you load your module:

    ```
    beforeEach(module('chapter5'));
    ```

3. Create a `beforeEach` function to inject the necessary dependencies and create a new scope instance and assign the artist to a scope:

    ```
    beforeEach(inject(function ($rootScope, $compile) {
      scope = $rootScope.$new();
      scope.artist = artist;
    }));
    ```

4. Next, within the `beforeEach` function, add the following code to create an Angular element providing the directive HTML string:

```
element = angular.element('<writers></writers>');
```

5. Compile the element providing our scope object:

```
$compile(element)(scope);
```

6. Now, call `$digest` on scope to simulate the scope life cycle:

```
scope.$digest();
```

7. Finally, to confirm whether these steps work as expected, write a simple test that uses the `text()` method available on the Angular element. The `text()` method will return the text contents of the element, which we then match against our artist value:

```
it('should display correct text in the DOM', function() {
   expect(element.text()).toBe('Graffiti artist: ' +
artist);
});
```

Here is what your code should look like to run the final test:

```
var scope;
var element;
var artist;

beforeEach(module('chapter5'));

beforeEach(function() {
   artist = 'Amara Por Dios';
});

beforeEach(inject(function($compile) {
   element = angular.element('<writers></writers>');
   scope.artist = artist;
   $compile(element)(scope);
   scope.$digest();
}));

it('should display correct text in the DOM', function() {
     expect(element.text()).toBe('Graffiti artist: ' +
artist);
});
```

How it works...

In step 4, the directive HTML tag is provided as a string to the `angular.element` function. The angular element function wraps a raw DOM element or an HTML string as a jQuery element if jQuery is available; otherwise, it defaults to using Angular's jQuery lite which is a subset of jQuery. This wrapper exposes a range of useful jQuery methods to interact with the element and its content (for a full list of methods available, visit `https://docs.angularjs.org/api/ng/function/angular.element`).

In step 6, the element is compiled into a template using the `$compile` service. The `$compile` service can compile HTML strings into a template and produces a template function. This function can then be used to link the scope and the template together. Step 6 demonstrates just this, linking the scope object created in step 3. The final step to getting our directive in a testable state is in step 7 where we call `$digest` to simulate the scope life cycle. This is usually part of the AngularJS life cycle within the browser and therefore needs to be explicitly called in a test-based environment such as this, as opposed to end-to-end tests using Protractor.

There's more...

One `beforeEach()` method containing the logic covered in this recipe can be used as a reference to work from for the rest of this chapter:

```
beforeEach(inject(function($rootScope, $compile) {
  // Create scope
  scope = $rootScope.$new();
  // Replace with the appropriate HTML string
  element = angular.element('<deejay></deejay>');
  // Replace with test scope data
  scope.deejay = deejay;
  // Compile
  $compile(element)(scope);
  // Digest
  scope.$digest();
}));
```

See also

- ▸ The *Setting up templateUrl* recipe
- ▸ The *Searching elements using selectors* recipe
- ▸ The *Accessing basic HTML content* recipe
- ▸ The *Accessing repeater content* recipe
- ▸ The *Scope changes based on user input* recipe

- ▶ The *Scope changes based on DOM events* recipe
- ▶ The *Class changes based on window properties* recipe

Setting up templateUrl

It's fairly common to separate the template content into an HTML file that can then be requested on demand when the directive is invoked using the `templateUrl` property. However, when testing directives that make use of the `templateUrl` property, we need to load and preprocess the HTML files to AngularJS templates. Luckily, the AngularJS team preempted our dilemma and provided a solution using Karma and the `karma-ng-html2js-preprocessor` plugin. This recipe will show you how to use Karma to enable us to test a directive that uses the `templateUrl` property.

Getting ready

For this recipe, you will need to ensure the following:

1. You installed Karma by following the *Installing Karma* recipe in *Chapter 1, Setup and Configuration*.

2. You installed the `karma-ng-html2js-preprocessor` plugin by following the instructions at `https://github.com/karma-runner/karma-ng-html2js-preprocessor/blob/master/README.md#installation`.

3. You configured the `karma-ng-html2js-preprocessor` plugin by following the instructions at `https://github.com/karma-runner/karma-ng-html2js-preprocessor/blob/master/README.md#configuration`.

4. Finally, you'll need a directive that loads an HTML file using `templateUrl` and for this example, we apply a scope value to the element in the DOM. Consider the following example:

```
angular.module('chapter5', [])
  .directive('emcees', function() {
    return {
      restrict: 'E',
      templateUrl: 'template.html',
      link: function(scope, element) {
        scope.emcee = scope.emcees[0];
      }
    };
  })
```

An example template could be as simple as what we will use for this example (`template.html`):

```
<h1>{{emcee}}</h1>
```

How to do it...

1. First, create three variables accessible across all tests:
   - One for the element: `var element;`
   - One for the scope: `var scope;`
   - One for some dummy data to assign to a scope value: `var emcees = ['Roxanne Shante', 'Mc Lyte'];`

2. Next, ensure that you load your module:
   ```
   beforeEach(module('chapter5'));
   ```

3. We also need to load the actual template. We can do this by simply appending the filename to the `beforeEach` function we just created in step 2:
   ```
   beforeEach(module('chapter5', 'template.html'));
   ```

4. Next, create a `beforeEach` function to inject the necessary dependencies and create a new scope instance and assign the artist to a scope:
   ```
   beforeEach(inject(function ($rootScope, $compile) {
     scope = $rootScope.$new();
     Scope.emcees = emcees;
   }));
   ```

5. Within the `beforeEach` function, add the following code to create an Angular element providing the directive HTML string:
   ```
   element = angular.element('<emcees></emcees>');
   ```

6. Compile the element providing our scope object:
   ```
   $compile(element)(scope);
   ```

7. Call `$digest` on scope to simulate the scope life cycle:
   ```
   scope.$digest();
   ```

8. Next, create a basic test to establish that the text contained within the `h1` tag is what we expect:
   ```
   it('should set the scope property id to the correct initial
   value', function () {});
   ```

9. Now, retrieve a reference to the h1 tag using the `find()` method on the element providing the tag name as the selector:

```
var h1 = element.find('h1');
```

10. Finally, add the expectation that the h1 tag text matches our first emcee from the array we provided in step 4:

```
expect(h1.text()).toBe(emcees[0]);
```

11. You will see the following passing test within your console window:

```
funkdoc:chapter_5 newtriks$ karma start
INFO [karma]: Karma v0.12.23 server started at http://localhost:9876/
INFO [launcher]: Starting browser Chrome
INFO [Chrome 38.0.2125 (Mac OS X 10.10.0)]: Connected on socket QCgT4jUkZuqovVYGS39_ with id 15606525
Chrome 38.0.2125 (Mac OS X 10.10.0): Executed 1 of 1 SUCCESS (0.045 secs / 0.042 secs)
```

How it works...

The `karma-ng-html2js-preprocessor` plugin works by converting HTML files into JS strings and generates AngularJS modules that we load in step 3. Once loaded, AngularJS makes these modules available by putting the HTML files into the `$templateCache`. There are libraries available to help incorporate this into your project build process, for example using Grunt or Gulp. There is a popular example specifically for Gulp at `https://github.com/miickel/gulp-angular-templatecache`. Now that the template is available, we can access the HTML content using the compiled element we created in step 5.

In this recipe, we access the text content of the element using the `find()` method. Be aware that if using the smaller jQuery lite subset of jQuery, there are certain limitations compared to the full-blown jQuery version. The `find()` method in particular is limited to look up by tag name only. To read more about the `find()` method, visit the jQuery API documentation at `http://api.jquery.com/find`.

See also

▸ The *Starting with testing directives* recipe

Searching elements using selectors

Directives, as you should know, attach special behavior to a DOM element. When AngularJS compiles and returns the element on which the directive is applied, it is wrapped by either **jqLite** or jQuery. This exposes an API on the element, offering many useful methods to query the element and its contents. In this recipe, you will learn how to use these methods to retrieve elements using selectors.

Getting ready

Follow the logic to define a `beforeEach()` function with the relevant logic to set up a directive as outlined in the *Starting with testing directives* recipe in this chapter. For this recipe, you can replicate the template that I suggested in the first recipe's *There's more...* section. For the purpose of this recipe, I tested against a property on scope named `deejay`:

```
var deejay = {
  name: 'Shortee',
  style: 'turntablism'
};
```

You can replace this with whatever code you have within the directive you're testing.

How to do it...

1. First, create a basic test to establish that the HTML code contained within an h2 tag is as we expected:

    ```
    it('should return an element using find()', function ()
    {});
    ```

2. Next, retrieve a reference to the h2 tag using the `find()` method on the element providing the tag name as the selector:

    ```
    var h2 = element.find('h2');
    ```

3. Finally, we create an expectation that the element is actually defined:

    ```
    expect(h2[0]).toBeDefined();
    ```

How it works...

In step 2, we use the `find()` method with the `h2` selector to test against in step 3's expectation. Remember, the element returned is wrapped by jqLite or jQuery. Therefore, even if the element is not found, the object returned will have jQuery-specific properties; this means that we cannot run an expectation on the element alone being defined. A simple way to determine if the element itself is indeed defined is to access it via jQuery's internal array of DOM objects, typically the first. So, this is why in our recipe we run an expectation against `element[0]` as opposed to `element` itself.

There's more...

► Here is an example using the `querySelector()` method. The `querySelector()` method is available on the actual DOM so we need to access it on an actual HTML element and not the jQuery wrapped element. The following code shows the selector we use in a CSS selector:

```
it('should return an element using querySelector and css
selector', function() {
  var elementByClass = element[0].querySelector('.deejay-
style');
  expect(elementByClass).toBeDefined();
});
```

► Here is a another example using the `querySelector()` method that uses an `id` selector:

```
it(should return an element using querySelector and id selector',
function() {
  var elementByClass = element[0].querySelector(' #deejay_name');
  expect(elementByClass).toBeDefined();
});
```

You can read more about the `querySelector()` method at `https://developer.mozilla.org/en-US/docs/Web/API/document.querySelector`.

See also

► The *Starting with testing directives* recipe

► The *Accessing basic HTML content* recipe

Accessing basic HTML content

A substantial number of directive tests will involve interacting with the HTML content within the rendered HTML template. This recipe will teach you how to test whether a directive's HTML content is as expected.

Getting ready

Follow the logic to define a `beforeEach()` function with the relevant logic to set up a directive as outlined in the *Starting with testing directives* recipe in this chapter. For this recipe, you can replicate the template that I suggested in the first recipe's *There's more...* section. For the purpose of this recipe, I will test against a property on a scope named `deejay`:

```
var deejay = {
  name: 'Shortee',
  style: 'turntablism'
};
```

You can replace this with whatever code you have within the directive you're testing.

How to do it...

1. First, create a basic test to establish that the HTML code contained within a h2 tag is as we expected:

   ```
   it('should display correct deejay data in the DOM',
   function () {});
   ```

2. Next, retrieve a reference to the h2 tag using the `find()` method on the element providing the tag name as the selector:

   ```
   var h2 = element.find('h2');
   ```

3. Finally, using the `html()` method on the returned element from step 2, we can get the HTML contents within an expectation that the h2 tag HTML code matches our scope's `deejay` name:

   ```
   expect(h2.html()).toBe(deejay.name);
   ```

How it works...

We made heavy use of the jQuery (or jqLite) library methods available for our element. In step 2, we use the `find()` method with the h2 selector. This returns a match for us to further utilize in step 3, in our expectation where we access the HTML contents of the element using the `html()` method this time (http://api.jquery.com/html/).

There's more...

We could also run a similar expectation for text within our h2 element using the `text()` method (`http://api.jquery.com/text/`) on the element, for example:

```
it('should retrieve text from <h2>', function() {
  var h2 = element.find('h2');
  expect(h2.text()).toBe(deejay.name);
});
```

See also

- ▶ The *Starting with testing directives* recipe
- ▶ The *Searching elements using selectors* recipe

Accessing repeater content

AngularJS facilitates generating repeated content with ease using the `ngRepeat` directive. In this recipe, we'll learn how to access and test repeated content.

Getting ready

Follow the logic to define a `beforeEach()` function with the relevant logic to set up a directive as outlined in the *Starting with testing directives* recipe in this chapter. For this recipe, you can replicate the template that I suggested in the first recipe's *There's more...* section. For the purpose of this recipe, I tested against a property on scope named `breakers`:

```
var breakers = [{
  name: 'China Doll'
}, {
  name: 'Crazy Legs'
}, {
  name: 'Frosty Freeze'
}];
```

You can replace this with whatever code you have within the directive you're testing.

How to do it...

1. First, create a basic test to establish that the HTML code contained within the h2 tag is as we expected:

   ```
   it('should display the correct breaker name', function ()
   {});
   ```

2. Next, retrieve a reference to the `li` tag using the `find()` method on the element providing the tag name as the selector:

```
var list = element.find('li');
```

3. Finally, targeting the first element in the list, we retrieve the text content expecting it to match the first item in the breakers array:

```
expect(list.eq(0).text()).toBe('China Doll');
```

How it works...

In step 2, the `find()` method using `li` as the selector will return all the list items. In step 3, using the `eq()` method (http://api.jquery.com/eq/) on the returned element from step 2, we can get the HTML contents at a specific index, zero in this particular case. As the returned object from the `eq()` method is a jQuery object, we can call the `text()` method, which immediately after that will return the text content of the element. We can then run an expectation that the first `li` tag text matches the first breaker within the scope array.

See also

▸ The *Starting with testing directives* recipe

▸ The *Searching elements using selectors* recipe

▸ The *Accessing basic HTML content* recipe

Scope changes based on user input

This recipe will show you how to update the scope using the user's input. There is a slight potential overlap in this recipe where it could be interpreted that we are testing AngularJS logic, which the AngularJS team would have already comprehensively covered in their test suites. However, I would justify this by stating that we are testing a specific element, which when interacted with in a particular manner, updates a specific value on the scope. By the end of this recipe, you will be familiar with interacting with a directive, updating the content of an element, and then triggering an event to update the scope. Finally, we will test whether the value on the scope matches what we expected.

Getting ready

For this example, I have a simple directive that contains an input field and binds to a key press event. If the key pressed is the *Enter* key, then the value of the input field is added to the array of `breakers`:

```
directive('breakers', function() {
  return {
    restrict: 'E',
    template: '<input type="text" name="input" value="" ng-
    keypress="onSubmit($event)"><ul><li ng-repeat="breaker
    in breakers">{{breaker.name}}</li></ul>',
    link: function(scope) {
      scope.onSubmit = function(event) {
        if (event.which === 13) {
          var input = event.target;
          scope.breakers.push({name:input.value});
        }
      }
    }
  };
})
```

Follow the logic to define a `beforeEach()` function with the relevant logic to set up a directive as outlined in the *Starting with testing directives* recipe in this chapter. For this recipe, you can replicate the template that I suggested in the first recipe's *There's more...* section. For the purpose of this recipe, I will test against a property on the scope named breakers that I will assign an empty array:

```
var breakers = [];
```

You can replace this with whatever code you have within the directive you're testing.

How to do it...

1. First, create a `beforeEach()` function that will inject the `$controller` service to register a new instance of a controller named `HomeCtrl` and also provide the scope object that we created in the *Getting ready* section of this recipe:

```
beforeEach(inject(function($controller) {
  $controller('HomeCtrl', {
    $scope: scope
  });
}));
```

2. Next, create a basic test that will ensure that the scope was updated as expected:

```
it('should update breakers list with defined input value',
function () {});
```

3. Next, create a small helper function that returns the first HTML element in the directive template:

```
function $input() {
  return element.children().eq(0);
}
```

4. Next, use the helper function from step 3 to target the input field and using the `val()` method, set the input value to the first breaker from our array:

```
$input().val('China Doll');
```

5. Manually trigger our key-press event by calling the `onSubmit()` method and pass an object with the minimal information required to satisfy the handler's requirements:

```
// Trigger submit using Enter key
scope.onSubmit({
  which: 13,
  preventDefault: function() {},
  target: $input()[0]
});
```

6. Finally, run the expectation on the first value's name property on our breakers array matching against the value we set in step 4:

```
expect(scope.breakers[0].name).toBe('China Doll');
```

How it works...

In step 4, using the power of jqLite (or jQuery), we are able to set the value of the input field with the `val()` method (`http://api.jquery.com/val/`). At this point, we have populated the input and now need to trigger the key-press handler with the relevant data to ensure that its value gets pushed on to our array in step 5. Triggering the key-press event is as easy as calling the `onSubmit()` method on scope, yet we need to ensure that we pass the information required by the event handler:

1. The `which` property: The `onSubmit()` handler only processes key events triggered by the *Enter* key. We determine the key press using the jQuery `which` property (`http://api.jquery.com/event.which/`) that normalizes `event.keyCode` and `event.charCode`. The enter key reports as 13.

2. The `preventDefault` property: This is called by the handler in our directive. Providing an empty function will suffice to satisfy this dependency.

3. The `target` property: This is required so the handler can retrieve the input value.

4. This now results in a valid event being passed to the scope handler with the required data to ensure that a value gets added to the breakers array and therefore ensure that the expectation in step 6 passes.

- ▸ The *Starting with testing directives* recipe
- ▸ The *Searching elements using selectors* recipe

Scope changes based on DOM events

Window events are easy to listen and respond to using the `bind()` method available on an element. One such case can be responsive layouts based on window size. In this recipe, we will run through how to test changes to scope based on window events, specifically the resize event.

Getting ready

For this example, I have a simple directive that binds to the `$window` resize event. On resizing, the `$window outerWidth` parameter is assigned to a scope property:

```
directive('writers', function($window) {
  return {
    restrict: 'E',
    link: function(scope, element) {

      function onResize(e) {
        scope.windowWidth = $window.outerWidth;
        scope.$digest();
      }

            angular.element($window).bind('resize',
            onResize);
      }
    };
});
```

Follow the logic to define a `beforeEach()` function with the relevant logic to set up a directive as outlined in the *Starting with testing directives* recipe in this chapter. For this recipe, you can replicate the template that I suggested in the first recipe's *There's more...* section. You can replace this with whatever code you have within the directive you're testing.

How to do it...

1. First, create a `beforeEach()` function that will inject the `$window` service, which we assign to a variable:

```
var $window;
beforeEach(inject(function(_$window_) {
  $window = _$window_;
}));
```

2. Next, create a basic test that will ensure that the scope was updated as expected:

```
it('should update scope with current window width on window
resize', function () {});
```

3. Using the `$window` service, call its `resizeTo()` method by passing in a width and height value `100`:

```
$window.resizeTo(100, 100);
```

4. Next, create a small helper function that dispatches an event, for example:

```
function dispatchEvent(type) {
  var evt = document.createEvent('Event');
  evt.initEvent(type, true, true);
  $window.dispatchEvent(evt);
}
```

5. Use the helper function from step 4 to dispatch a resize event:

```
dispatchEvent('resize');
```

6. Finally, run the expectation on the `windowWidth` scope property matching it against our defined window width value of `100` from step 3:

```
expect(scope.windowWidth).toBe(100);
```

How it works...

We use the `$window` service as opposed to the browser's window object for testability. The AngularJS `$window` service allows overriding, mocking, and so on, which for testing, proves to be indispensable. In step 3, we call the `resizeTo()` method on the `$window` service, which does what it says on the tin. In step 4, we define a function that steps through creating a custom event that gets dispatched by our `$window` service. The function expects one argument, which is the event type so we can reuse this function in other tests if required. Step 5 uses the `dispatchEvent()` method passing `resize` as the argument. Our directive will handle this event and assign the new window width to scope. Step 6 validates this logic for us.

There's more...

Remember the DRY (http://en.wikipedia.org/wiki/Don't_repeat_yourself) principle within your tests. An example within this code is the extraction of the dispatch event logic into its own function. Another small improvement we can make to this recipe (and others in this book) is to assign values used for testing to variables. This also means that when it comes to changing any values, you will have minimized the number of locations that require updating. Within this recipe, we can change the width and height values to variables, for example:

```
var width = 100;
var height = 100;
it('should update scope with current window width on window resize',
function() {
  $window.resizeTo(width, height);
  dispatchEvent('resize');
  expect(scope.windowWidth).toBe(width);
});
```

See also

- ▸ The *Starting with testing directives* recipe
- ▸ The *Searching elements using selectors* recipe

Class changes based on window properties

The ngClass module allows you to dynamically set CSS classes on an HTML element using data binding. To do this, an expression is evaluated on each of the classes you wish to add. In this recipe, we will test whether a specific class is added to an element based on a window property.

Getting ready

For this example, I have a small directive that makes use of ngClass to conditionally apply a class named popup. The isPopup property on scope determines the condition by using the search() method (https://developer.mozilla.org/en-US/docs/Web/JavaScript/Reference/Global_Objects/String/search) on the $window.name property (https://developer.mozilla.org/en-US/docs/Web/API/Window.name). The search() method returns a string index greater than -1 if it matches our regular expression for popup on the $window.name object:

```
directive('deejay', function($window) {
  return {
    restrict: 'E',
    template: '<div class="deejay-booth" ng-class="{popup: isPopup
    === true}"></div>',
    link: function(scope) {
      scope.isPopup = $window.name.search(/popup/) >= 0;
    }
  };
})
```

Follow the logic to define a `beforeEach()` function with the relevant logic to set up a directive as outlined in the *Starting with testing directives* recipe in this chapter. For this recipe, you can replicate the template that I suggested in the first recipe's *There's more...* section. You can replace this with whatever code you have within the directive you're testing.

How to do it...

1. First, create a beforeEach() function that will inject the `$window` service, which we then assign to a variable:

    ```
    Var $window;
    beforeEach(inject(function(_$window_) {
        $window = _$window_;
    }));
    ```

2. Next, create a basic test that will ensure that the scope was updated as expected:

    ```
    it('should have specific popup class if window name contains
    popup', function () {});
    ```

3. Retrieve a reference to the `div` class first using the `find()` method on the element providing the div tag name as the selector, and then using the `attr()` method to retrieve CSS classes on the returned element:

    ```
    var divClasses = element.find('div').attr('class');
    ```

4. Next, set the `$window.name` object to the `popup` value:

    ```
    $window.name = 'popup';
    ```

5. Finally, check for the popup value in the `divClasses` string from step 3:

    ```
    expect(divClasses).toContain('popup');
    ```

How it works...

Using the `find()` method, we can search for the `div` element. We then use the `attr()` method (`http://api.jquery.com/attr/`) on the returned `div` element to get the value of the class attribute. This returns a string of all the CSS classes. In step 4, using the `$window` service, we are able to set the name property to our test value. In step 5, we used the `toContain` matcher to search the CSS classes' string for the `popup` string.

There's more...

We can use the `split()` method (`https://developer.mozilla.org/en-US/docs/Web/JavaScript/Reference/Global_Objects/String/split`) on the string of classes providing a regular expression to split the string based on whitespace. This would return an array of class names that we could interrogate further in our tests or use the same `toContain()` matcher with the same results:

```
expect(divClasses.split(/\s+/g)).toContain('popup');
```

See also

- The *Starting with testing directives* recipe
- The *Searching elements using selectors* recipe

Directive changes on interaction using Protractor

As your directives flourish and begin to direct actions influencing the UI or state, Protractor will give you a silent nod to encourage you to step up. In this recipe, the directive logic itself is a doddle and the e2e tests are far from elaborate. However, they are a foundation you can build on as your directives become more intricate. In this recipe, we will use Protractor to test hiding and showing an HTML element based on a user clicking a button.

Getting ready

For this example, I have a directive that displays a deejay's information. Within the main `div` is a button that when clicked changes a scope property called `showBooth` to false. The `showBooth` value is used by the `ngShow` module, which is an attribute on the main div:

```
directive('deejay', function($window) {
  return {
    restrict: 'E',
    template: '<div ng-show="showBooth" class="deejay-
    booth"><h2 id="deejay_name">{{deejay.name}}</h2><p
    class="deejay-style">{{deejay.style}}</p><button
    class="hide-btn" ng-click="hideBooth()">Hide
    Booth</button></div>',
    link: function(scope) {
      scope.showBooth = true;

      scope.hideBooth = function() {
        scope.showBooth = false;
      };
    }
  };
})
```

Ensure that you have Protractor installed and running. You also need to make sure that your project is running on a local server so that Protractor can load the webpage and run the application. In this example, I have used `localhost port 8000`, however you can amend this according to your development environment.

How to do it...

1. Firstly, use the `get` method to load the page by passing the URL to the local development server that is running our application:

```
beforeEach(function () {
  browser.get('http://0.0.0.0:8000/');
});
```

2. Next, create a test stating our intention that the HTML element is displayed first:

```
it('should show content on page load', function () {});
```

3. Select the element that has the `ngShow` attribute:

```
Var deejayBooth = $('[ng-show=showBooth].deejay-booth');
```

4. Add an expectation that the element we selected is actually displayed:

```
expect(deejayBooth.isDisplayed()).toBeTruthy();
```

5. Next, create a test stating our intention that the HTML element is not displayed when the hide button is clicked:

```
it('should hide content on button click', function () {});
```

6. Within the test from step 5, select the element that has the `ngShow` attribute:

   `Var deejayBooth = $('[ng-show=showBooth].deejay-booth');`

7. Using a jQuery selector, call the `click()` method on the hide button:

   `$('.hide-btn').click();`

8. Now, add an expectation that the element we selected is actually displayed:

   `expect(deejayBooth.isDisplayed()).toBeFalsy();`

How it works...

In step 3 and 6, we use the jQuery attribute equals selector (`http://api.jquery.com/attribute-equals-selector/`) providing the attribute value of `ng-show` and an additional CSS selector specific to the `div` we are targeting. Before we test our logic to hide the element, we first ensure that it is displayed; this is demonstrated in step 4. Once we confirm this, it is actually displayed. We trigger the click event (`http://api.jquery.com/click/`) on the button element in step 7.

See also

- ▸ The *Installing Protractor recipe* in *Chapter 1, Setup and Configuration*
- ▸ The *Searching elements using selectors* recipe

6

Using Spies to Test Events

In this chapter, you will learn the following recipes:

- ▶ Testing event dispatches
- ▶ Testing the handling of dispatched events
- ▶ Testing the handling of external events
- ▶ Testing the handling of callbacks
- ▶ Testing events using Protractor

Introduction

As your AngularJS applications grow in size, you'll inevitably separate the code into multiple modules. A great reference to guide you on the modularity of an AngularJS application can be found at `https://github.com/johnpapa/angularjs-styleguide#modularity`. To help facilitate the communication between modules without sharing the scope, you can use events. The event concept in AngularJS, however, is not as intelligible as we would hope and therefore testing can sometimes become overly complex when it need not be.

 I recommend that you read the following excellent article at `http://toddmotto.com/all-about-angulars-emit-broadcast-on-publish-subscribing` to help you gain a deeper understanding of Angular's event system.

This chapter will try and lift the veil on some of the techniques behind testing events and hopefully provide some fundamentals for your future application development.

Testing event dispatches

Broadcasting events in AngularJS are dispatched down the `$scope` hierarchy as opposed to `$emit` dispatching it upwards. Regardless of direction, we need to test whether an event was actually dispatched and for this chapter we will favor the `$broadcast` method (`https://docs.angularjs.org/api/ng/type/$rootScope.Scope#$broadcast`). The `$broadcast` method requires a name and one or more optional arguments, which will be passed on to all the event listeners.

This recipe will show you how to test broadcasting events from an AngularJS controller using Jasmine spies (`http://jasmine.github.io/2.0/introduction.html#section-Spies`). The core goal initially is to determine whether a specific method broadcasts an event. We then go into further depth to analyze whether the correct data is broadcasted. It's important to understand here that we are not testing AngularJS logic such as testing whether the `$broadcast` method functions as we would expect, rather than testing whether the event is dispatched at our specified prompt with the correct name and data.

Getting ready...

For this recipe, you simply need logic that broadcasts an event, such as within a controller. As an example, here is the code to get you started with testing in this recipe, which basically defines a method on the scope that we can call from within our test. The method dispatches an event named `showWuEmcee` using the `$broadcast` method. A string from the scope method argument is also dispatched as a single argument for the event:

```
var HomeCtrl = function($scope) {
  $scope.showWuEmcee = function(emceeName) {
    $scope.$broadcast('showWuEmcee', emceeName);
  };
};
```

How to do it...

1. Create a variable for `scope` and another for an array of string values to use within the test:

```
var scope;
var wuTangClan = ['RZA', 'GZA', 'Method Man', 'Raekwon',
'Ghostface Killah', 'Inspectah Deck', 'U-God', 'Masta
Killa', 'Cappadonna', 'ODB'];
```

2. Next, ensure that you load your module:

```
beforeEach(module('chapter6'));
```

3. Write a `beforeEach` function to inject the necessary dependencies and create a new scope instance:

```
beforeEach(inject(function ($rootScope, $controller) {
  scope = $rootScope.$new();
}));
```

4. Within the `beforeEach` function from step 3, register a new instance of a controller named `HomeCtrl` providing the scope object created in step 3:

```
beforeEach(inject(function ($rootScope, $controller) {
  scope = $rootScope.$new();
  $controller('HomeCtrl', {
    $scope: scope
  });
}));
```

5. Within the `beforeEach` function again, create a new spy on the scope object and stub the `$broadcast` method:

```
beforeEach(inject(function ($rootScope, $controller) {
  scope = $rootScope.$new();
  $controller('HomeCtrl', {
    $scope: scope
        });
  spyOn(scope, '$broadcast');
}));
```

6. Next, create a test to establish that our spy was called:

```
it('should call $broadcast', function() {});
```

7. Within the test created in step 6, call the `showWuEmcee` method on scope that should broadcast an event:

```
scope.showWuEmcee();
```

8. Finally, add an expectation that the `$broadcast` spy was called:

```
expect(scope.$broadcast).toHaveBeenCalled();
```

How it works...

A super simple way to determine whether an event was broadcasted at a defined moment is accomplished using Jasmine spies. In step 5, we created a spy to stub the `$broadcast` method on scope. Jasmine proxies the object to allow expectations to be made on its invoked methods. In step 7, we call the `showWuEmcee` method that should broadcast our event. In step 8, we create an expectation that uses the `toHaveBeenCalled` matcher that returns `true` if the spy was called.

There's more...

Testing whether the event was broadcasted is the groundwork we can build on to delve deeper and test broadcasting further:

1. Let's test whether the event was dispatched with the correct name and argument using the `toHaveBeenCalledWith` matcher. This returns true if the argument list matches any of the recorded calls to the spy:

```
it('should call $broadcast with correct event name and emcee',
function() {
  scope.showWuEmcee(wuTangClan[0]);
  expect(scope.$broadcast).toHaveBeenCalledWith('showWuEmcee',
wuTangClan[0]);
});
```

2. Next, let's use the `calls` property (http://jasmine.github.io/2.0/ introduction.html#section-Other_tracking_properties) and test whether first argument contains the first item in the array created in step 1 of this recipe:

```
it('should call $broadcast with specific argument', function() {
  scope.showWuEmcee(wuTangClan[0]);
  expect(scope.$broadcast.calls.argsFor(0)).toContain(wuTangC
  lan[0]);
});
```

See also...

> ▸ The *Testing the handling of dispatched events* recipe

Testing the handling of dispatched events

After dispatching an event, we can safely surmise that there is a function out there somewhere listening for and responding to it. To listen for events in AngularJS, we use the `$on` method and supply it with the name of the event it should listen out for and an event handler function.

This recipe guides you on how to test the handling of a dispatched event and ensures that the necessary processes that our handler performs are executed as expected. Just to clarify, we are not checking AngularJS's specific logic where a broadcasted (or emitted) event calls a listener; we are testing whether the handler function we stipulate responds as we envisaged and successively runs the expected logic.

Getting ready...

For this recipe, you will need an example of broadcasting an event, for example within a controller and an associated listener. As an example, we build on the example shown in the *Getting ready* section of the *Testing event dispatches* recipe and add a listener and function to call when the event is dispatched. Obviously, dispatching and listening for an event in the same controller is not the brightest of ideas but it serves well for demonstration purposes:

- ▶ The dispatched event we listen for using the `$on` method is `showWuEmcee`.

- ▶ Our handler function is a method on `$scope` named `onShowWuEmcee`.

- ▶ Within the `onShowWuEmcee` method, we assign different values to the `$scope` property `wuWho` based on whether the value supplied is undefined or not:

```
var HomeCtrl = function($scope) {
  $scope.UNKNOWN_NAME = 'Unknown emcee';
  $scope.showWuEmcee = function(emceeName) {
    $scope.$broadcast('showWuEmcee', emceeName);
  };
  $scope.onShowWuEmcee = function(e, emceeName) {
    if (!emceeName) {
      $scope.wuWho = $scope.UNKNOWN_NAME;
      return;
    }
    $scope.wuWho = emceeName;
  }
  $scope.$on('showWuEmcee', $scope.onShowWuEmcee);
};
```

How to do it...

1. First, create a variable for scope and another for an array of string values to use within the test:

```
var scope;
var wuTangClan = ['RZA', 'GZA', 'Method Man', 'Raekwon',
'Ghostface Killah', 'Inspectah Deck', 'U-God', 'Masta Killa',
'Cappadonna', 'ODB'];
```

2. Next, ensure that you load your module:

```
beforeEach(module('chapter6'));
```

3. Write a `beforeEach` function to inject the necessary dependencies and create a new scope instance:

```
beforeEach(inject(function ($rootScope, $controller) {
  scope = $rootScope.$new();
}));
```

4. Next, within the `beforeEach` function from step 3, register a new instance of a controller named `HomeCtrl` providing the scope object created in step 3:

```
$controller('HomeCtrl', {
  $scope: scope
});
```

5. Create a test to establish that the value assigned to scope is equal to the provided `emceeName` object:

```
it('should assign correct emcee to scope', function() {});
```

6. Next, within the test created in step 5, broadcast the `showWuEmcee` event and a value from our test array created in step 1:

```
scope.$broadcast('showWuEmcee', wuTangClan[1]);
```

7. Finally, add an expectation that the `scope.wuWho` value is equal to the value provided in step 6:

```
expect(scope.wuWho).toEqual(wuTangClan[1]);
```

How it works...

In step 6, we broadcast an event with the name `showWuEmcee` along with a single argument, which is a value from our test array created in step 1. Step 7 raises an expectation that `scope.wuWho` is equal to the value we broadcasted, `wuTangClan[1]`.

There's more...

In the preceding steps, we tested one area of logic from our example function; that scope updates to the value provided by the broadcasted event. Let's now test the logic that a default value gets assigned to scope if the broadcasted event does not provide any data, that is `emceeName` is undefined.

1. First, create a test to establish that a default value is assigned to the scope if the `emceeName` is undefined:

```
it('should assign default emcee to scope if emceeName
undefined ', function() {});
```

2. Within the test created in step 1, broadcast the `showWuEmcee` event:

```
scope.$broadcast('showWuEmcee');
```

3. Next, add an expectation that the `scope.wuWho` value is equal to `scope.NO_NAME` (a default value):

```
expect(scope.wuWho).toEqual(scope.NO_NAME);
```

See also...

▶ The *Testing event dispatches* recipe

Testing the handling of external events

AngularJS provides a multitude of useful directives that enable us to simply handle events, however, not all DOM events are nicely wrapped into directives for us. Additionally, there may be third-party or external events that need to be handled.

AngularJS's jqLite provides us with a method to make it straightforward to attach to a DOM element and handle events that it dispatches. This wondrous method is known simply as `on()` (http://api.jquery.com/on/) and is accessible on AngularJS elements (https://docs.angularjs.org/api/ng/function/angular.element). The `on()` method accepts a string naming the event type and a handler function.

 Be aware of the jqLite limitations of the `on()` method. It does not support namespaces, selectors, or `eventData` functions.

This recipe will demonstrate how to test responding to a DOM event that makes use of the `on()` method.

Getting ready...

For this recipe, you'll need to have attached the `on()` method to an external event and updated a scope property within the event handler. Here is the code as an example for testing that uses the `on()` method on the `$window` service listening for the `oncanplay` event and updating `scope.canPlay` to `true`:

```
directive('wuTang', function($window) {
  return {
    restrict: 'A',
    link: function(scope, element) {
      scope.canPlay = false;
      angular.element($window).on('oncanplay', function() {
        scope.canPlay = true;
      });
    }
  };
})
```

How to do it...

1. First, create a variable for scope and another for an AngularJS element:

```
var scope;
var element;
```

2. Next, ensure that you load your module:

```
beforeEach(module('chapter6'));
```

3. Write a `beforeEach` function to inject the necessary dependencies and create a new scope instance:

```
beforeEach(inject(function ($rootScope, $compile) {
  scope = $rootScope.$new();
}));
```

4. Next, within the `beforeEach` function from step 3, add the following code to create an AngularJS element providing the attribute directive HTML string:

```
element = angular.element('<div wu-tang></div>');
```

5. Within the `beforeEach` function from step 3, compile the element providing our scope object:

```
$compile(element)(scope);
```

6. Within the `beforeEach` function from step 3, call `$digest` on scope to simulate the scope's life cycle:

```
scope.$digest();
```

7. Next, create a small helper function that dispatches an event:

```
function dispatchEvent(type) {
  var evt = document.createEvent('Event');
  evt.initEvent(type, true, true);
  window.dispatchEvent(evt);
}
```

8. Create a test to establish that the value assigned to the scope is equal to updates based on a DOM event:

```
it('should respond to an event and update scope',
function() {});
```

9. Now, use the helper function from step 7 to dispatch a `oncanplay` event:

```
dispatchEvent('oncanplay');
```

10. Next, add an expectation that the `scope.canPlay` value is true:

```
expect(scope.canPlay).toBeTruthy();
```

How it works...

There are only two steps that reproduce the behavior of the window dispatching an `oncanplay` event, which our code should be listening for, and handling. Our little helper function in step 7 enables us to easily use the window object to dispatch a custom event. Step 9 makes use of the helper function to create and dispatch an event of the `oncanplay` type. Step 10 simply tests whether the scope value has been updated to true.

See also...

► The *Testing the handling of dispatched events* recipe

Testing the handling of callbacks

There are many third-party JavaScript components available for integration into your AngularJS application. Many will expose some sort of API that may include methods specific to events related to the component. An example of such a component is the **JW player** (`http://www.jwplayer.com`).

The JW player API has an `onReady()` method available that expects a callback as an argument. I have come across many convoluted approaches to testing this scenario, including intricate mocks and complex spies. In this recipe, I will show you how to test the callback workflow that components such as JW player provide (hint: it's easier than you might think).

Getting ready...

Our primary goal is to test a third-party component that makes use of callbacks. The JW player has been chosen for this recipe as it's a popular JS library with an extensive API making use of callbacks. It would be great if you have a project that makes use of the JW player. However, if you do not have such a project and want to get started with this recipe, we can quickly create a factory service (`https://docs.angularjs.org/api/auto/service/$provide#factory`) as shown here. We create a factory named `jwplayer` that follows a rough imitation of how the JW player API can be targeted. The service returns a single method called `onReady` that returns a provided callback:

```
factory('jwplayer', function() {
  return function() {
    return {
      onReady: function(callback) {
        return callback;
      }
    }
  };
})
```

Here is a directive called `jwplayer` that performs the following tasks:

- Sets `scope.ready` initially to false
- Instantiates a new instance of our `jwplayer` service
- Provides a callback to the `onReady` method
- Within the callback, updates `scope.ready` to true:

```
directive('jwplayer', function(jwplayer) {
  return {
    restrict: 'EA',
    link: function(scope, element) {
      scope.ready = false;

      jwplayer()
      .onReady(scope.readyHandler);

      scope.readyHandler = function() {
        scope.ready = true;
      }
    }
  };
})
```

How to do it...

1. First, create a variable for the scope and another for `element`:
    ```
    var scope;
    var element
    ```

2. Next, ensure that you load your module:
    ```
    beforeEach(module('chapter6'));
    ```

3. Write a `beforeEach` function to inject the necessary dependencies and create a new scope instance:
    ```
    beforeEach(inject(function ($rootScope, $compile) {
      scope = $rootScope.$new();
    }));
    ```

4. Within the `beforeEach` function from step 3, add the following code to create an AngularJS element providing the directive HTML string:
    ```
    element = angular.element('<jwplayer></ jwplayer>');
    ```

5. Within the `beforeEach` function from step 3, compile the element providing our scope object:

   ```
   $compile(element)(scope);
   ```

6. Next, within the `beforeEach` function from step 3, call `$digest` on the scope to simulate the scope's life cycle:

   ```
   scope.$digest();
   ```

7. Create a test to establish that the value assigned to the scope is updated:

   ```
   it('should update scope within callback', function() {});
   ```

8. Next, call the `readyHandler()` method on the scope:

   ```
   scope.readyHandler();
   ```

9. Add an expectation that the `scope.playing` function is true:

   ```
   expect(scope.ready).toBeTruthy();
   ```

How it works...

The key to testing callbacks, such as this JW player example, is predictably not the test code. It's how we approach the application code itself using a scope property for the callback handler. This simple approach enables us to isolate the handler and facilitate testing. We need not concern ourselves with the JW player, nor its API. We can trigger our callback within the test as it's accessible on the scope object and this is exactly what we do in step 8.

Testing events using Protractor

To truly feel confident with your event-driven processes, you need to start testing within the browser using the trusty Protractor. Protractor will help coax out those potential cross-browser inconsistencies we have all grown to love and cherish. This recipe will guide you on testing expected distinct UI changes based on interactive events, for example clicking specific DOM elements.

Getting ready...

For this example, I have a directive that loads an HTML template. The template contains a couple of button type input, which on click action, will create a style setting to fill using specific colors, for example, `ng-click="wuStyle={'fill':'red'}"`. Ensure that you have Protractor installed and running. You also need to make sure that your project is running on a local server so that Protractor can load the web page and run the application. In this example, I use localhost port 8000, however, you can amend this according to your development environment.

How to do it...

1. Use the `get` method to load the page by passing the URL to the local development server running our application:

    ```
    beforeEach(function () {
      browser.get('http://0.0.0.0:8000/');
    });
    ```

2. Next, create a test stating our intention that the HTML element is displayed first:

    ```
    it('should update the wu logo background color following
    click events', function () {});
    ```

3. Select the logo using the ID as the selector:

    ```
    var logo = $('#logo');
    ```

4. Add an expectation that the logo background initial fill is black:

    ```
    expect(logo.getCssValue('fill')).toBe('rgb(0, 0, 0)');
    ```

5. Using the `by.css()` selector, find the input with a value of red and call the `click()` method:

    ```
    element(by.css('input[value=red]')).click();
    ```

6. Next, add an expectation that the logo background fill is now red:

    ```
    expect(logo.getCssValue('fill')).toBe('rgb(255, 0, 0)');
    ```

7. Using the `by.css()` selector, find the input with a value of blue and call the `click()` method:

    ```
    element(by.css('input[value=blue]')).click();
    ```

8. Next, add an expectation that the logo background fill is now blue:

    ```
    expect(logo.getCssValue('fill')).toBe('rgb(0, 0, 255)');
    ```

How it works...

In steps 3 and 6, we use the jQuery attribute equals selector (http://api.jquery.com/attribute-equals-selector/) providing the attribute value of ng-show and an additional CSS selector specific to the `div` tag we are targeting. Before we test our logic to hide the element, we first ensure that it is displayed, which is demonstrated in step 4. Once we confirm that it is actually displayed, we trigger the click event (http://api.jquery.com/click/) on the button element in step 7.

See also...

▶   The *Installing Protractor* recipe in *Chapter 1, Setup and Configuration*

7
Testing Filters

In this chapter, you will learn the following recipes:

- ▸ Testing a filter that formats a number as text
- ▸ Testing a filter that formats seconds to a time string
- ▸ Using Protractor to test filter changes based on input
- ▸ Using Protractor to test filter changes based on events

Introduction

Filters are used to format input data and output the result to be displayed to the user. Filters are easily integrated into an AngularJS application via view templates or within controllers, services, and so on. AngularJS provides the `$filter` service (`https://docs.angularjs.org/api/ng/service/$filter`) that uses the `$filterProvider` API (`https://docs.angularjs.org/api/ng/provider/$filterProvider`) and executes a filter when the input changes. The typical expectation, we can assume, for the use of filters is to format some information into either an easy-to-comprehend presentation of the data, or a recognized (or potentially approved) representation. Therefore, testing whether a filter functions as expected is crucial to your application. Incorrect formatting can lead to confusing or inaccurate representation of your data within the UI. Testing filters focuses on input and output, thus keeps test logic simple and fairly standard across most filters you'll encounter. This chapter will give you direction on getting started with testing filters, both as standalone unit tests and as integrated end-to-end tests using Protractor.

Testing a filter that formats a number as text

In this recipe, you will learn how to test a filter that returns the value of a number rounded to the nearest integer. This recipe will demonstrate how effortlessly you can test a filter based on input and filtered output.

Getting ready

You can adapt this recipe and use the number filter AngularJS provides (`https://docs.angularjs.org/api/ng/filter/number`) or you can use the custom filter I provided based on the example that Mozilla provides at `https://developer.mozilla.org/en-US/docs/Web/JavaScript/Reference/Global_Objects/Math/round`.

Following are the steps for this recipe's example:

1. Register a filter named `decimalAdjust` with your application module:

   ```
   .filter('decimalAdjust', function() {
   });
   ```

2. Next, within the function from step 1, write a function that expects the type of adjustment, the number, and the exponent:

   ```
   return function(type, value, exp) {};
   ```

3. Finally, write the logic within the function from step 2 that adjusts and returns the value:

   ```
   // If the exp is undefined or zero...
   if (typeof exp === 'undefined' || +exp === 0) {
       return Math[type](value);
   }
   value = +value;
   exp = +exp;
   // If the value is not a number or the exp is not an
   integer...
   if (isNaN(value) || !(typeof exp === 'number' && exp % 1 === 0)) {
       return NaN;
   }
   // Shift
   value = value.toString().split('e');
   value = Math[type](+(value[0] + 'e' + (value[1] ?
   (+value[1] - exp) : -exp)));
   // Shift back
   ```

```
value = value.toString().split('e');
return +(value[0] + 'e' + (value[1] ? (+value[1] + exp) :
exp));
```

Also ensure that you've loaded your module, for example:

```
beforeEach(module('chapter7'));
```

How to do it...

1. First, create a variable for the filter we are testing:

   ```
   var decimalAdjustFilter;
   ```

2. Next, write a `beforeEach` function to inject the `$filter` service and retrieve our filter function assigning it to the variable created in step 1:

   ```
   beforeEach(inject(function ($filter) {
     decimalAdjustFilter = $filter('decimalAdjust');
   }));
   ```

3. Create a test to establish that our filter works as expected:

   ```
   it('should adjust decimal correctly using round',
   function() {});
   ```

4. Finally, within the test created in step 3, add an expectation that the number our filter function returns matches the value we provided:

   ```
   expect(decimalAdjustFilter('round', 55.55, -1)).toBe(55.6);
   ```

How it works...

As you can see, testing filters is not a complicated process. In step 2, we gain access to our filter using the `$filter` service providing our filter name (`decimalAdjust`) as the sole argument. In step 4, we call and provide the filter with the obligatory arguments and use the `toBe` matcher to determine test success or failure.

See also

- ▸ The *Testing a filter that formats seconds to a time string* recipe
- ▸ The *Using Protractor to test filter changes based on events* recipe
- ▸ The *Using Protractor to test filter changes based on input* recipe

Testing a filter that formats seconds to a time string

In this recipe, you will learn how to test a filter that accepts input of a number and outputs a string. The numeric input for this example is a time value in seconds and is formatted to a time string, HH:MM:SS.

Getting ready

Here is an example filter that converts seconds into time-based text that you can use as a reference for this recipe:

1. First, register a filter named `secondsToTime` with your application module:

```
.filter('secondsToTime', function() {
});
```

2. Next, within the function from step 1, write a function that expects the seconds value as an argument:

```
return function(value) {};
```

3. Finally, write the logic within the function from step 2 that calculates and returns a formatted time string:

```
var seconds = Math.floor(value % 60).toString();
var minutes = Math.floor(value / 60 % 60).toString();
var hours = Math.floor(value / 60 / 60 % 24).toString();
function pad(t) {
  if (t && t.length < 2) {
    return '0' + t;
  }
  return t;
}
return pad(hours > 0 ? hours.concat(':') :
'').concat(pad(minutes), ':', pad(seconds));
```

Also ensure you've loaded your module, for example:

```
beforeEach(module('chapter7'));
```

How to do it...

1. First, create a variable for the filter we are testing:

```
var secondsToTimeFilter;
```

2. Next, write a `beforeEach` function to inject the `$filter` service and retrieve our filter function assigning it to the variable created in step 1:

```
beforeEach(inject(function ($filter) {
  secondsToTimeFilter = $filter('secondsToTime');
}));
```

3. Now, create a test to establish that our filter works as expected:

```
it('should return a time formatted string (seconds)',
function() {});
```

4. Finally, within the test created in step 3, add an expectation that the string our filter function returns matches the value we provided:

```
expect(secondsToTimeFilter(1)).toBe('00:01');
```

How it works...

As mentioned in the introduction to this chapter, the logic to testing filters is fairly consistent. In step 2, we gain access to our filter using the `$filter` service providing `secondsToTime` as the solitary argument. In step 4, we provide the filter with the seconds value and use the `toBe` matcher to determine whether the test succeeds or fails by returning the formatted time string.

There's more...

Based on the preceding example, we can easily test minutes and hours; here is the code that can be added to achieve results in seconds or minutes:

- Minutes: `expect(secondsToTimeFilter(103)).toBe('01:43');`
- Hours: `expect(secondsToTimeFilter(9504)).toBe('2:38:24');`

See also

- The *Testing a filter that formats a number as text* recipe
- The *Using Protractor to test filter changes based on events* recipe
- The *Using Protractor to test filter changes based on input* recipe

Using Protractor to test filter changes based on input

This recipe will show you how to use Protractor to test data that is filtered following user input. First, we will simulate entering data into an input field and then click the button to filter the value.

Getting ready

In this example, you need to have an input field to enter a decimal number that will be rounded by our filter. The filter needs to by applied based on a user action, for example when a button is clicked. We use the *Testing a filter that formats a number as text* recipe's example code to test within this recipe.

Ensure that you have Protractor installed and running and if you need guidance on setting up Protractor, please read the *Installing Protractor* recipe in *Chapter 1*, *Setup and Configuration*. Please update your URL and port based on your configuration.

How to do it...

1. Firstly, we need to ensure that Protractor navigates our browser to the correct URL, that is, our local server and port:

   ```
   beforeEach(function () {
     browser.get('http://0.0.0.0:8000/');
   });
   ```

2. Next, create a test stating our intention that the HTML displays the correct decimal value:

   ```
   it('should display the correct decimal value', function
   () {});
   ```

3. Find the filter button, by text using the buttonText method:

   ```
   var button = element(by.buttonText('Filter'));
   ```

4. Next, find the decimal input text field:

   ```
   var decimalText = element(by.model('decimal'));
   ```

5. Clear the text field:

   ```
   decimalText.clear();
   ```

6. Now, populate the text field with a decimal:

   ```
   decimalText.sendKeys('55.55');
   ```

7. Next, call the `click()` method on the button element:

   ```
   button.click();
   ```

8. Finally, add an expectation that the text field has been updated to reflect the formatted number:

   ```
   expect(decimalText.getAttribute('value')).toBe('55.6');
   ```

How it works...

In step 3, we use the `buttonText` locator (`http://angular.github.io/protractor/#/api?view=ProtractorBy.prototype.buttonText`) to find the filter button. In step 4, we use the model locator (`http://angular.github.io/protractor/#/api?view=ProtractorBy.prototype.model`) to find the text input element. In step 5, we ensure that the text field is empty by using the clear method (`http://angular.github.io/protractor/#/api?view=webdriver.WebElement.prototype.clear`) prior to step 6 where we type a sequence of keys into the input field using the `sendKeys` method (`http://angular.github.io/protractor/#/api?view=webdriver.WebElement.prototype.sendKeys`). In step 7, we use the click method (`http://angular.github.io/protractor/#/api?view=webdriver.WebElement.prototype.click`) on our button element to filter the input from step 6.

See also

▶ The *Testing a filter that formats a number as text* recipe

▶ The *Testing a filter that formats seconds to a time string* recipe

▶ The *Using Protractor to test filter changes based on events* recipe

▶ The *Installing Protractor* recipe in *Chapter 1, Setup and Configuration*

Using Protractor to test filter changes based on events

In this recipe, we'll test the output of a filter from repeatedly executed code using the `setInterval` method. The `setInterval` method is started and stopped by a user action (button click). The filter function will take numeric seconds as input and output a time string that we will test to check whether it matches the expected format. A few use case examples for this logic come to my mind, for example, a video playback time event or a stopwatch. For this example, I will take the stopwatch scenario.

Getting ready

Seeing as there's a little more overhead to the application setup I will provide the example code to get you up and running quicker:

1. First, register a directive that injects the `secondsToTimeFilter` filter we used in the *Testing a filter that formats seconds to a time string* recipe's example:

```
.directive('stopWatch', function(secondsToTimeFilter) {
  return {
    require: 'ngModel',
    link: function(scope) {}
  };
});
```

2. Within the link function from step 2, use the following logic that starts and stops our stopwatch:

```
var timerInterval;
var timerOffset;

scope.timer = {
  current: 0,
  running: false
};

scope.start = function() {
  timerOffset = Date.now();
  timerInterval = setInterval(scope.update, 10);
};

scope.update = function() {
  scope.timer.current += scope.delta();
  scope.$digest();
};

scope.stop = function() {
    clearInterval(timerInterval);
};

scope.delta = function() {
  var now = Date.now();
  var delta = now - timerOffset;
  timerOffset = now;
```

```
    return delta;
  };

  // Listeners
  scope.onStartTimer = function() {
    scope.timer.running = !scope.timer.running;
    if (scope.timer.running) {
      scope.start();
    } else {
      scope.stop();
    }
  };

  scope.onResetTimer = function() {
      scope.timer.current = 0;
  };
```

3. Next, add the following HTML making use of our `stop-watch` directive as an attribute, a span tag to display the formatted string, and buttons to start/stop and reset the stopwatch:

```
<div stop-watch ng-model="timer">
    <span>{{timer.current | secondsToTime}}</span>
    <button ng-click="onStartTimer()">{{!timer.running &&
'Start' || 'Stop'}}</button>
    <button ng-click="onResetTimer()">Reset</button>
</div>
```

Ensure that you have Protractor installed and running, and if you need guidance on setting up Protractor, please read the *Installing Protractor* recipe in *Chapter 1*, *Setup and Configuration*. Please update your URL and port based on your configuration.

How to do it...

1. Firstly, we need to ensure that Protractor navigates our browser to the correct URL, that is, our local server and port:

```
beforeEach(function () {
  browser.get('http://0.0.0.0:8000/');
});
```

2. Next, create a test stating our intention that the HTML displays the correct formatted time:

```
    it('should display the correct time format', function ()
    {});
```

3. Find the start/stop button, using the `buttonText` method:

```
var button = element(by.partialButtonText('St'));
```

4. Find the element displaying the time using the `binding` method:

```
var timeText = element(by.binding('timer.current'));
```

5. Now, start the stopwatch calling the `click()` method on the button element:

```
button.click();
```

6. Stop the stopwatch calling the `click()` method on the button element:

```
button.click();
```

7. Finally, add an expectation that the `timeText` text displayed has the correct format using a regular expression:

```
expect(timeText.getText()).toMatch(/^([01]?[0-9]|2[0-
3]):[0-5][0-9]$/);
```

How it works...

Due to the stopwatch button toggling its label between start and stop, to find that particular button element we need to use the `partialButtonText` locator (`http://angular.github.io/protractor/#/api?view=ProtractorBy.prototype.partialButtonText`), as shown in step 3. In step 4, we use the binding locator (`http://angular.github.io/protractor/#/api?view=ProtractorBy.prototype.binding`) to find the element that will display the formatted time. In step 5 and step 6, we use the `click()` method to start and stop the stopwatch. Finally, we use a regular expression (credits to `http://www.mkyong.com/regular-expressions/how-to-validate-time-in-24-hours-format-with-regular-expression`) as a matcher to ensure that the text displays the correctly formatted time string.

See also

- ▶ The *Testing a filter that formats a number as text* recipe
- ▶ The *Testing a filter that formats seconds to a time string* recipe
- ▶ The *Using Protractor to test filter changes based on input* recipe
- ▶ The *Installing Protractor* recipe in *Chapter 1, Setup and Configuration*

8
Service and Factory Testing with Mocks and Spies

In this chapter, you will learn the following recipes:

- ▸ Getting started with testing a service
- ▸ Testing HTTP GET requests using $httpBackend
- ▸ Testing HTTP POST requests using $httpBackend
- ▸ Using spies to test HTTP GET requests
- ▸ Using spies to test HTTP POST requests
- ▸ Testing service data using mock helpers
- ▸ Testing rejected $http promises
- ▸ Testing constants
- ▸ Using Protractor to test HTTP requests

Introduction

Services (`https://docs.angularjs.org/guide/services`) are typically used to assemble and transmit data throughout your application. They may be used to compute values or form a communication channel with external resources, requesting data and dispatching the responses back into the application. Services are singleton objects and are relatively easy to test due to their segregation from core application logic. AngularJS is a popular choice when developing client-side applications that are rich in data. These applications are not concerned with storing large record sets of data and are commonly known to query RESTful APIs for data (`http://en.wikipedia.org/wiki/Representational_state_transfer`). Whether you're using a value, factory, or a service (further clarification on the definitions for these can be found at `http://stackoverflow.com/a/15666049`), you'll find that testing of computed data is covered elsewhere in this book.

In this chapter, we will primarily concentrate on testing services that generate HTTP requests using the `$http` service (`https://docs.angularjs.org/api/ng/service/$http`). This chapter will demonstrate various approaches to testing the $http service, both with spies and the `$httpBackend` service (`https://docs.angularjs.org/api/ngMock/service/$httpBackend`). As you work through this chapter (and the book) you'll begin to notice repetition in the test specs. The API for Jasmine is not vast and there are repeated patterns to configure AngularJS within your test suite. This will become even more evident in this chapter as you work through each recipe, requiring only minor tweaks in implementation to resolve test expectations.

This chapter will use the `$httpBackend` service to test GET and POST requests. Services, as with many other aspects of AngularJS applications, can be approached in a variety of ways based on developers' preferences and coding techniques. The majority of recipes in this chapter concentrate on the testing of the request within a service and try to avoid focusing too much on how the request is invoked. We will test rejected promises, a constant service, and how to extend Jasmine to mock data facilitating reuse throughout test specs. This chapter focuses on GET and POST requests; once you've nailed the specifics for these methods, testing various other methods will be a cinch.

Getting started with testing a service

In this recipe, we'll simply test a service that exposes an API method as expected. Then, throughout the rest of this chapter, we will build on this foundation to start testing logic within the actual service itself.

Getting ready

All that is required for this recipe is a straightforward service with a method, which we will verify is defined. For this recipe, I have a service named `emcees` and a method named `getUKEmcees`:

```
.service('emcees', function() {
  return {
    getUKEmcees: function() {}
  };
});
```

Also, ensure that you've loaded your module:

```
beforeEach(module('chapter8'));
```

How to do it...

Follow these steps to determine whether a service API method named `getUKEmcees` is defined:

1. First, create a variable for the service we are testing:

   ```
   var emcees;
   ```

2. Next, write a `beforeEach` function to inject the `$injector` service and retrieve our service, assigning it to the variable created in step 1:

   ```
   beforeEach(inject(function($injector) {
     emcees = $injector.get('emcees');
   }));
   ```

3. Now, create a test to demonstrate that our service is accessible and exposes a method:

   ```
   it('should have a method defined', function() {});
   ```

4. Finally, within the test created in step 3, add an expectation that the `getUKEmcees` service method is defined:

   ```
   expect(emcees.getUKEmcees).toBeDefined();
   ```

How it works...

Using the `$injector` service's `get` method in step 2, we inject our `emcees` service and assign it to a variable for reuse throughout the rest of the spec. In step 4, we simply provide the `expect` function with a reference to the `getUKEmcees` method expecting it to be defined in our `emcees` service. This is a modest example that serves as a basis to start testing the API that your service exposes.

See also

- ▸ The *Testing HTTP GET requests using $httpBackend* recipe
- ▸ The *Testing HTTP POST requests using $httpBackend* recipe
- ▸ The *Using spies to test HTTP GET requests* recipe
- ▸ The *Using spies to test HTTP POST requests* recipe
- ▸ The *Testing service data using mock helpers* recipe
- ▸ The *Testing rejected $http promises* recipe

Testing HTTP GET requests using $httpBackend

This recipe will demonstrate how to use the $httpBackend service to test whether an HTTP GET request is made when a method exposed by a service is invoked. You'll learn how to inject and use the $httpBackend service to return custom responses from a GET request. This serves as a basis that you can expand on to test how your services handle different types of data responses.

Getting ready

For this recipe, a service is required with a method exposed that, when called, makes an HTTP GET request. For this recipe, I use an example service named emcees and a method named getUKEmcees. The service makes use of the $http service's get() method (https://docs.angularjs.org/api/ng/service/$http#get) that returns a **promise** with two methods specific to $http: success and error, as shown in the following code:

```
.service('emcees', function($http) {
  return {
    getUKEmcees: function() {
      return $http.get('/emcees/uk');
    }
  };
});
```

Also, ensure that you've loaded your module; consider the following example:

```
beforeEach(module('chapter8'));
```

How to do it...

Follow these steps to test whether our service makes the HTTP GET request:

1. Create three variables, one for the service we are testing, another for the $httpBackend service, and the last for a reference to a URL that we will use throughout the recipe:

```
var emcees;
var $httpBackend;
var url;
```

2. Next, write a beforeEach function to inject the $injector, and retrieve and assign our services to the variables created in step 1. Also, define a URL to test the service:

```
beforeEach(inject(function($injector) {
  emcees = $injector.get('emcees');
  $httpBackend = $injector.get('$httpBackend');
  url = '/emcees/uk';
}));
```

3. Next, within the beforeEach function in step 2, use the $httpBackend service to respond to HTTP GET with some mock data:

```
$httpBackend.when('GET', url).respond({
  data: ['kamanchi-sly', 'el-eye', 'rola']
});
```

4. Write an afterEach function calling the relevant methods to verify that all HTTP requests were made and there are none to be flushed:

```
afterEach(function() {
  $httpBackend.verifyNoOutstandingExpectation();
  $httpBackend.verifyNoOutstandingRequest();
});
```

5. Create a test such that our service makes a GET request:

```
it('should make a GET request', function() {});
```

6. Create a new request expectation for a GET request providing the URL we defined in step 2:

```
$httpBackend.expectGET(url);
```

7. Next, call the getUKEmcees method on our service:

```
emcees.getUKEmcees();
```

8. Finally, flush all pending requests:

```
$httpBackend.flush();
```

How it works...

In step 3, we specified a backend definition using the `when` method on the `$httpBackend` service. The `when` method expects an HTTP method as its first argument; we provide a value of `GET` and then the URL defined in step 2 as the method's second argument. The `when` method returns an object with a `respond` method allowing us to control how to handle the matched request. Finally, in step 3, we respond with some mock data to replace what we would expect from a real server response.

In step 4, the `afterEach` function verifies that all HTTP requests were made and there are none to be flushed. This is a great additional coverage to ensure that stipulated HTTP expectations are fulfilled and will fail tests accordingly. The `expectGET` method in step 6 creates a new request expectation for `GET` requests. We provide the URL defined in step 2 and the expectation will return `true` if the URL matches the current definition.

Step 8 is the final key move where we make use of the `flush` method, a pitfall newcomers to AngularJS can encounter. This wondrous method enables us to have the best of both the asynchronous and synchronous worlds by explicitly flushing pending requests.

See also

- The *Getting started with testing a service* recipe in this chapter
- The *Testing HTTP POST requests using $httpBackend* recipe in this chapter
- The *Using spies to test HTTP GET* requests recipe
- The *Using spies to test HTTP POST* requests recipe
- The *Testing service data using mock helpers* recipe
- The *Test rejected $http promises* recipe

Testing HTTP POST requests using $httpBackend

This recipe will demonstrate how to use `$httpBackend` to test whether an HTTP `POST` request is made when a method exposed by a service is invoked. You will learn how to create a new backend definition for a `POST` request validating that the correct URL and POST data is passed to the service method and mock a response.

Getting ready

For this recipe, a service is required with a method exposed that, when called, makes an HTTP POST request. Here, I use an example service named emcees and a method named addUKEmcee:

```
.service('emcees', function($http) {
  return {
    addUKEmcee: function(emcee) {
      return $http.post('/emcees/uk', emcee);
    }
  };
});
```

Also, ensure that you've loaded your module; consider the following example:

```
beforeEach(module('chapter8'));
```

How to do it...

1. First, create three variables, one for the service we are testing, another for the $httpBackend service, and the last for a reference to a URL that we will use throughout the recipe:

   ```
   var emcees;
   var $httpBackend;
   var url;
   ```

2. Next, write a beforeEach function to inject the $injector service, retrieve and assign our services to the variables created in step 1. Also, define a URL to test the service:

   ```
   beforeEach(inject(function ($injector) {
     emcees = $injector.get('emcees');
     $httpBackend = $injector.get('$httpBackend');
     url = '/emcees/uk';
   }));
   ```

3. Write an afterEach function calling the relevant methods to verify that all HTTP requests were made and there are none to be flushed:

   ```
   afterEach(function() {
       $httpBackend.verifyNoOutstandingExpectation();
       $httpBackend.verifyNoOutstandingRequest();
   });
   ```

4. Create a test such that our service makes a POST request:

```
it('should make a POST request', function() {});
```

5. Create a dummy object to be sent as part of the POST request:

```
var emcee = {
  'name': 'ids'
};
```

6. Next, create a new backend definition for a POST request with a simple response of a 201 HTTP status:

```
$httpBackend.expectPOST(url, emcee).respond(201, '');
```

7. Call the addUKEmcee method on our service providing the emcee object from step 5:

```
emcees.addUKEmcee(emcee);
```

8. Finally, flush all pending requests:

```
$httpBackend.flush();
```

How it works...

The *Testing HTTP GET requests using $httpBackend* recipe in this chapter explains some of the fundamental logic involved in using the mock HTTP backend implantation. When testing a POST as opposed to a GET request, we also need to provide data in the request message's body, data that we mock in step 5.

In step 6, we use the mock data as the second argument when we create a new backend definition for the POST request. We respond with an HTTP status code of 201 (http://www. w3.org/Protocols/rfc2616/rfc2616-sec10.html) to replace what we would expect from a real server response. The expectation will return true if both the URL and the data matches.

See also

- ▶ The *Getting started with testing a service* recipe in this chapter
- ▶ The *Testing HTTP GET requests using $httpBackend* recipe in this chapter
- ▶ The *Using spies to test HTTP GET requests* recipe in this chapter
- ▶ The *Using spies to test HTTP POST requests* recipe in this chapter
- ▶ The *Testing service data using mock helpers* recipe in this chapter
- ▶ The *Testing rejected $http promises* recipe in this chapter

Using spies to test HTTP GET requests

We have made great use of spies throughout this book, and the fun continues while testing services. Spies serve as a great way to easily test HTTP requests, and using spies to test services also maintains consistency in your overall application testing.

The aim of this recipe is to demonstrate how to mock the $http service and test whether a GET method was made with a spy.

Getting ready

For this recipe, a service is required with a method exposed that, when called, makes an HTTP GET request. Here, I use an example service named emcees and a method named getUKEmcees:

```
.service('emcees', function($http) {
  return {
    getUKEmcees: function() {
      return $http.get('/emcees/uk');
    }
  };
});
```

Also, ensure that you've loaded your module, for example:

```
beforeEach(module('chapter8'));
```

How to do it...

Follow the following steps to test whether a GET request is made using spies:

1. Create a variable for the service we are testing:

   ```
   var emcees;

   var httpMock;
   ```

2. Next, write a beforeEach function to load our mock module and inject the $provide service in an initialization function:

   ```
   beforeEach(module('cookbook', function($provide) {}));
   ```

3. Within the initialization function, create a new spy object providing the $http service as the object name to mock and the get method that will be created as a spy:

   ```
   httpMock = jasmine.createSpyObj('$http', ['get']);
   ```

4. Next, use the `$provide` service to register our newly created spy object with the `$http` service:

```
$provide.value('$http', httpMock);
```

5. Write a `beforeEach` function to inject the `$injector` service and retrieve our service, assigning it to the variable created in step 1:

```
beforeEach(inject(function($injector) {
    emcees = $injector.get('emcees');
}));
```

6. Next, create a test such that our service makes a GET request:

```
it('should make a GET request', function() {});
```

7. Call the `getUKEmcees` method on our service:

```
emcees.getUKEmcees();
```

8. Finally, create an expectation so that our spy GET method is called:

```
expect(httpMock.get).toHaveBeenCalled();
```

How it works...

The overall aim is to mock the `$http` service, entirely replacing the dependency on making an actual request. In step 3, the `$http` service mock is created using the Jasmine `createSpyObj` object and we then use the `$provide` service to register it with the injector in step 4.

To spy on a method on the mock object, we pass an array to `createSpyObj` with the name of the method, for example GET. In step 7, we call our `getUKEmcees` method on our service on which we expect to make a GET request. Step 8 confirms that this in an expectation asserting that our `$http` service mock had its GET method called.

There's more...

We can be more explicit about this request and ensure that the correct URL was requested. The following example uses the `toHaveBeenCalledWith` matcher that will return `true` if the argument provided to the `get()` method matches our expected URL /emcees/uk:

```
expect(httpMock.get).toHaveBeenCalledWith('/emcees/uk');
```

See also

▶ The *Getting started with testing a service* recipe in this chapter

▶ The *Testing HTTP GET requests using $httpBackend* recipe in this chapter

- ▸ The *Testing HTTP POST requests using $httpBackend* recipe in this chapter
- ▸ The *Using spies to test HTTP POST requests* recipe in this chapter
- ▸ The *Testing service data using mock helpers* recipe in this chapter
- ▸ The *Testing rejected $http promises* recipe in this chapter
- ▸ The *Mocking injected instances using spies* recipe in *Chapter 2, Getting Started with Testing and AngularJS*

Using spies to test HTTP POST requests

You will notice that spies are incredibly diverse and the simplicity of their implementation makes them a favorable choice when testing services. In this recipe, I will show you how to mock an $http service and test whether a POST method was made using a spy. You will also learn how to confirm that the data supplied is correct for the POST request using the toHaveBeenCalledWith method.

Getting ready

For this recipe, a service is required with a method exposed that, when called, makes an HTTP POST request. Here, I use an example service named emcees and a method named addUKEmcee:

```
.service('emcees', function($http) {
  return {
    addUKEmcee: function(emcee) {
      return $http.post('/emcees/uk', emcee);
    }
  };
});
```

Also, ensure that you've loaded your module, for example:

```
beforeEach(module('chapter8'));
```

How to do it...

1. Create three variables, one for the service we are testing, another for the HTTP mock, and the last for a reference to a URL that we will use throughout the recipe

```
var emcees;
var httpMock;
var url;
```

2. Next, write a `beforeEach` function to load our mock module and inject the `$provide` service in an initialization function:

```
beforeEach(module('cookbook', function($provide) {}));
```

3. Now, within the initialization function, create a new spy object providing the `$http` service as the object name to mock and the GET method that will be created as a spy:

```
httpMock = jasmine.createSpyObj('$http', ['post']);
```

4. Use the `$provide` service to register our newly created spy object with the `$http` service:

```
$provide.value('$http', httpMock);
```

5. Write a `beforeEach` function to inject the `$injector` service and retrieve and assign our services to the variables created in step 1. Also, define a URL to test the service:

```
beforeEach(inject(function ($injector) {
  emcees = $injector.get('emcees');
  url = '/emcees/uk';
}));
```

6. Next, create a test such that our service makes a POST request:

```
it('should make a POST request', function() {});
```

7. Create a dummy object to be sent as part of the POST request:

```
var emcee = {
  'name': 'alkaline'
};
```

8. Call the `addUKEmcee` method on our service providing the `emcee` object from step 5:

```
emcees.addUKEmcee(emcee);
```

9. Finally, create an expectation so that our spy `post` method is called:

```
expect(httpMock.post).toHaveBeenCalled();
```

How it works...

We mock the `$http` service in step 3 using the Jasmine createSpyObj method and spy on the `post` method. In step 4, we use the `$provide` service to register it with the injector. The data supplied to the POST request is created in, and sent as an argument for our service `addUKEmcee` method. Finally, in step 8, we confirm that our `$http` service mock had its POST method called.

There's more...

In this recipe, we supply an object to our service method, which is then sent as part of the POST request. Here, you will see how to confirm that the data supplied to the POST request is as expected:

1. Create a test such that our service makes a POST request with the correct data:

    ```
    it('should make a POST request with correct data',
    function() {});
    ```

2. Next, create a dummy object to be sent as part of the POST request:

    ```
    var emcee = {
      'name': 'tlp'
    };
    ```

3. Next, call the addUKEmcee method on our service providing the emcee object from step 5 in the preceding recipe:

    ```
    emcees.addUKEmcee(emcee);
    ```

4. Finally, create an expectation that our spy POST method was called with the expected URL and emcee data:

    ```
    expect(httpMock.post).toHaveBeenCalledWith(url, emcee);
    ```

Now that you know how to test the data sent in a request, you can modify and adapt this for services that transform data prior to a request.

See also

*   The *Getting started with testing a service* recipe in this chapter
*   The *Testing HTTP GET requests using $httpBackend* recipe in this chapter
*   The *Using spies to test HTTP GET requests* recipe in this chapter
*   The *Testing service data using mock helpers* recipe in this chapter
*   The *Testing rejected $http promises* recipe in this chapter
*   The *Mocking injected instances using an object* recipe in *Chapter 2, Getting Started with Testing and AngularJS*
*   The *Mocking injected instances using spies* recipe in *Chapter 2, Getting Started with Testing and AngularJS*

Testing service data using mock helpers

The *Using spies to test HTTP POST requests* recipe uses a mock data object to be sent along with the `POST` request. However, it's quite feasible that your application may repeatedly use specific objects in different locations, for example, sending within HTTP requests, or using as mock responses, and so on.

This can result in you mocking out the same (or similar) objects in multiple test files. There are different approaches that you can take to overcome this issue. In this recipe, you will see how to DRY (`http://en.wikipedia.org/wiki/Don%27t_repeat_yourself`) up some of your test code in the *Getting ready* section and then how to use this mock data in a test. In this recipe, you will also learn how to resolve a promise returned by the `$http` service, ensuring that the response data is set on our service object.

Getting ready

1. First, a service is required with a method exposed that, when called, makes an HTTP `GET` request. For this recipe, I use an example service named `emcees` and a method named `getUKEmcee` that requests an `emcee` using an `id` paramter. The `GET` response is then assigned to a property named `emcee` on the `emcees` service API:

    ```
    .service('emcees', function($http) {
      return {
        emcee: {},
        getUKEmcee: function(id) {
          var that = this;
          return $http.get('/emcees/uk/' + id)
          .then(function(response) {
            that.emcee = response;
          });
        }
      };
    });
    ```

2. Next, let's create our mock data file that we will use within this recipe test:

    -   First, create a file named `mockData.js` in the same directory as your test specs

    -   Next, within the file, add a new property to the Jasmine object named `mockData`:

        ```
        jasmine.mockData = (typeof jasmine.mockData ===
        'undefined') ? {} : jasmine.mockData;
        ```

□ Now, add a method named `emcee` to the `mockdata` object that returns some fake data that we will use in our test:

```
jasmine.mockData.emcee = function() {
  return {
    "name": "Spye",
    "crew": "Undivided Attention",
    "label": "Hairy Parents"
  };
};
```

3. Ensure that you've loaded your module, for example:

```
beforeEach(module('chapter8'));
```

How to do it...

1. Create variables that will be used throughout this test:

```
var emcees;
var httpMock;
var $q;
var $scope;
```

2. Next, write a `beforeEach` function to load our mock module and inject the `$provide` service in an initialization function:

```
beforeEach(module('cookbook', function($provide) {}));
```

3. Within the initialization function, create a new spy object providing the `$http` service as the object name to mock and the `get` method that will be created as a spy:

```
httpMock = jasmine.createSpyObj('$http', ['get']);
```

4. Next, use the `$provide` service to register our newly created spy object with the `$http` service:

```
$provide.value('$http', httpMock);
```

5. Now, write a `beforeEach` function to inject the `$injector` service and retrieve our service, assigning it to the variable created in step 1. Also, within this function, retrieve references to the `$q` service and create a new `$scope` object:

```
beforeEach(inject(function ($injector) {
        emcees = $injector.get('emcees');
        $q = $injector.get('$q');
        $scope = $injector.get('$rootScope').$new();
}));
```

6. Create a test to demonstrate that our service is accessible and exposes a method:

```
it('should store the response from the HTTP GET request',
function() {});
```

7. Create a reference to the promise instance by calling `defer` on the `$q` service:

```
var defer = $q.defer();
```

8. Next, create a local variable populated using the `emcee` method on the `mockData` object:

```
var emcee = jasmine.mockData.emcee();
```

9. Resolve our promise with the mock data from step 8:

```
defer.resolve(emcee);
```

10. Using the spy that we created in step 3, chain the spy with `and.returnValue` to return the promise instance:

```
httpMock.get.and.returnValue(defer.promise);
```

11. Next, call the `getUKEmcee` method on our service providing a value:

```
emcees.getUKEmcee('1');
```

12. Use `$scope.$digest` to process all the watchers:

```
$scope.$digest();
```

13. Finally, within the test created in step 6, add an expectation that the `emcee` object stored in our `emcees` service returns a value matching our mock data from step 8:

```
expect(emcees.emcee.name).toBe(emcee.name);
```

How it works...

Please refer to the *Using spies to test HTTP GET requests* recipe in this chapter, which explains the spy-related logic within this recipe. We started off with this recipe's *Getting ready* section by creating our mock data. In step 8, you can see how easily we reference that data using the global Jasmine object. The `$http` service returns a promise, and on a successful response, assigns the data to an object in our service.

We need that promise to resolve, which involves first grabbing a reference to the promise instance in step 7 and then resolving it with the mock data in step 9. In step 10, we stipulate that our spy method should return a specific value, which is our promise.

After progressing through calling our service and ensuring all watchers are processed in steps 11 and 12, we can then match the mock response against the service object data.

See also

▸ The *Getting started with testing a service* recipe in this chapter

▸ The *Testing HTTP GET requests using $httpBackend* recipe in this chapter

▸ The *Testing HTTP POST requests using $httpBackend* recipe in this chapter

▸ The *Using spies to test HTTP GET requests* recipe in this chapter

▸ The *Using spies to test HTTP POST requests* recipe in this chapter

▸ The *Testing rejected $http promises* recipe in this chapter

▸ The *Mocking injected instances using spies* recipe in *Chapter 2, Getting Started with Testing and AngularJS*

Testing rejected $http promises

In this recipe, we will address the unfortunate occurrence of an HTTP request returning an error. AngularJS uses promises (`https://docs.angularjs.org/api/ng/service/$q`), which offer a single point to handle errors that may arise from an HTTP request. The promise error handler, based on your application preference, can handle the error accordingly.

For example, you may want to dispatch an event with the error message or throw an actual JavaScript **Error** (`https://developer.mozilla.org/en-US/docs/Web/JavaScript/Reference/Global_Objects/Error`) that your application consumes and handles. For this recipe, I will choose the latter and reject a promise and then throw an error. We'll write a test to ensure that an error is thrown when our HTTP GET request is rejected.

Getting ready

A service is required with a method exposed that, when called, makes an HTTP GET request. For this recipe, I use an example service named emcees and a method named getUKEmcee that requests an emcee using an id value. Using the catch method on the promise API, we pass the error provided by the callback to throw an error:

```
.service('emcees', function($http) {
  return {
    getUKEmcee: function(id) {
      return $http.get('/emcees/uk/' + id)
      .catch(function(error) {
        throw Error(error);
      });
    }
  };
});
```

Ensure that you've loaded your module, for example:

```
beforeEach(module('chapter8'));
```

How to do it...

1. First, create a variable for the service we are testing:

    ```
    var emcees;
    var httpMock;
    var $q;
    var $scope;
    ```

2. Next, write a `beforeEach` function to load our mock module and inject the `$provide` service in an initialization function:

    ```
    beforeEach(module('cookbook', function($provide) {}));
    ```

3. Within the initialization function, create a new spy object providing the `$http` service as the object name to mock and the `get` method that will be created as a spy:

    ```
    httpMock = jasmine.createSpyObj('$http', ['get']);
    ```

4. Next, use the `$provide` service to register our newly created spy object with the `$http` service:

    ```
    $provide.value('$http', httpMock);
    ```

5. Now, write a `beforeEach` function to inject the `$injector` service and retrieve our service, assigning it to the variable created in step 1. Also, within this function, retrieve references to the `$q` service and create a new `$scope` object:

    ```
    beforeEach(inject(function ($injector) {
      emcees = $injector.get('emcees');
      $q = $injector.get('$q');
      $scope = $injector.get('$rootScope').$new();
    }));
    ```

6. Create a test to demonstrate that our service is accessible and exposes a method:

    ```
    it('should throw an error', function() {});
    ```

7. Create a reference to the promise instance by calling `defer` on the `$q` service:

    ```
    var defer = $q.defer();
    ```

8. Create an error message string:

    ```
    var errorMsg = 'Unauthorized';
    ```

9. Now, reject our promise with the error message from step 8:

    ```
    defer.reject(errorMsg);
    ```

10. Using the spy we created in step 3, chain the spy with `and.returnValue` to return the promise instance:

```
httpMock.get.and.returnValue(defer.promise);
```

11. Next, provide an anonymous function as a value for the `expect` function and use the `toThrowError` matcher expecting our error message:

```
expect(function() {}).toThrowError(errorMsg);
```

12. Call the `getUKEmcee` method on our service providing a value:

```
emcees.getUKEmcee('1');
```

13. Finally, use `$scope.$digest` to process all the watchers:

```
$scope.$digest();
```

How it works...

Please refer to the *Using spies to test HTTP GET requests* recipe, which explains the spy-related logic within this recipe. In step 7, we grab a reference to the promise that we reject in step 9 providing an error message defined in step 8. To test throwing errors using the `toThrowError` method from Jasmine, we need to provide the `expect` function with an anonymous function as seen in step 11. In steps 12 and 13, we add to the function and call our `service` method and ensure that all watchers are processed.

There's more...

If throwing an error within a catch handler in your application is not your preference, you can remove the `catch()` method in your service and then update the function we used in the recipe, as follows:

```
it('should catch a failure', function() {
  var errorMsg = 'Unauthorized';
  var defer = $q.defer();

  defer.reject(errorMsg);
  httpMock.get.and.returnValue(defer.promise);

  emcees.getUKEmcee('1').catch(function(error) {
    expect(error).toEqual(errorMsg);
  })
  $scope.$digest();
});
```

We now add the expectation to the `catch` method in our test and compare the error message that the promise returns to match our expected message.

See also

- ▶ The *Getting started with testing a service* recipe in this chapter
- ▶ The *Testing HTTP GET requests using $httpBackend* recipe in this chapter
- ▶ The *Using spies to test HTTP GET requests* recipe in this chapter
- ▶ The *Using spies to test HTTP POST* requests recipe in this chapter
- ▶ The *Testing service data using mock helpers* recipe in this chapter

Testing constants

This recipe is a quick and easy overview of how to test a constant service (`https://docs.angularjs.org/api/auto/service/$provide#constant`). Constants can be useful for a variety of reasons, ranging from defining responsive breakpoints, global strings for notifications/errors, or access keys to libraries such as `https://keen.io`. If you're interested in environment-based constants for configuration of your AngularJS application, ensure that you read my blog post at `http://newtriks.com/2013/11/29/environment-specific-configuration-in-angularjs-using-grunt/`, which makes use of a Yeoman generator I wrote called `env-config`. This recipe will show you how to test whether a constant has been defined and then take it further by testing whether it returns an object with a correct string value.

Getting ready

For this recipe, a constant service is required. As an example, here is what I use to test in this recipe, which defines a constant named `MESSAGES` and exposes an object with a property named `errors`. The value of `emcees` is an object containing properties with error string values:

```
.constant('MESSAGES', {
  'errors': {
    'ukemcees': 'There was an error loading emcees based in good old blighty.'
  }
});
```

Ensure that you've loaded your module, for example:

```
beforeEach(module('chapter8'));
```

How to do it...

1. First, create a variable for the service we are testing:

```
var MESSAGES;
```

2. Next, write a `beforeEach` function to inject the `MESSAGES` service and retrieve our service, assigning it to the variable created in step 1:

```
beforeEach(inject(function (_MESSAGES_) {
  MESSAGES = _MESSAGES_;
}));
```

3. Now, create a test to demonstrate that our service is accessible and exposes a method:

```
it('should have a MESSAGES constant object', function()
{});
```

4. Finally, within the test created in step 3, add an expectation that the service method `getUKEmcees` is defined:

```
expect(MESSAGES).toBeDefined();
```

How it works...

We first need to inject our constant service in step 2. The final step is easy; we match against the service being defined.

There's more...

We will take this recipe a little further and actually test whether a constant value is as we would expect. I will be completely honest and state that I can not justify one hundred percent the necessity to test constant values, but here we go:

1. Create a test to demonstrate that our service is accessible and exposes a method:

```
it('should have correct errors.http.ukemcees constant',
function() {});
```

2. Next, create a message that should match our constant string value:

```
var message = 'There was an error loading emcees based in
good old blighty.';
```

3. Finally, retrieve the value of `ukemcees` and match it against the message variable from step 2:

```
expect(MESSAGES.errors.ukemcees).toBe(message);
```

See also

▶ The *Getting started with testing a service* recipe in this chapter

Using Protractor to test HTTP requests

In this recipe, we will use Protractor to test the broader spectrum of events related to an HTTP request and ensure that our application UI updates are as expected. The school of thought I follow is that end-to-end tests should reflect the application in the closest state possible to its running in the production environment. This helps identify potential problems between client and server communication, which can be obscured using HTTP mocks.

I have known end-to-end tests to actually highlight a problem with the server API before any other potential source. If, however, you do not, or cannot, test against an actual server for HTTP requests, then AngularJS provides a fake backend implementation at `https://docs.angularjs.org/api/ngMockE2E/service/$httpBackend`, plus there are other modules that can be used to set up mocks for HTTP calls (`https://github.com/atecarlos/protractor-http-mock`).

For this recipe, we will use a fantastic fake online REST API called `JSONPlaceholder` (`http://jsonplaceholder.typicode.com`). You can also run `JSONPlaceholder` locally using npm (`https://www.npmjs.com/package/jsonplaceholder`); please refer to the main website for instructions on how to do this.

Getting ready

In this example, you need to have a button that, when clicked, will make an HTTP request and assign the response data as a collection on scope. In the HTML, the collection should be displayed using the `ng-repeat` directive (`https://docs.angularjs.org/api/ng/directive/ngRepeat`).

Here are the steps for the example code I use for this recipe's end-to-end testing:

1. In your HTML, add a button that calls a function on scope, and also a repeater as well:

```
<body ng-controller="HomeCtrl">
  <button ng-click="onLoadUsers()" ng-
  show="!users.length">Load Users</button>
    <div ng-repeat="user in users">
      <span>{{user.name}}</span>
    </div>
</body>
```

2. Create a controller that defines a handler for the button click and calls a service to request users:

```
var HomeCtrl = function($scope, users) {
  $scope.onLoadUsers = function() {
    users.getUsers().then(function(response) {
      $scope.users = response.data;
    });
  };
};
```

3. Create a service that makes a request to an API and returns suitable data to populate the repeater:

```
.service('users', function($http) {
  return {
    getUsers: function() {
      return
      $http.get('http://jsonplaceholder.typicode.com/users');
    }
  };
})
```

Ensure that you have Protractor installed and running and if you need guidance on setting up Protractor, please read the *Installing Protractor* recipe in *Chapter 1, Setup and Configuration*. Please update your URL and port based on your configuration.

How to do it...

1. Firstly, use the `get` method to load the page by passing the URL to the local development server running our application:

```
beforeEach(function () {
  browser.get('http://0.0.0.0:8000/');
});
```

2. Next, create a test stating our intention that the HTML displays users and hides the button to load users:

```
it('should do display users and hide the load users
button on success', function (){});
```

3. Find the load users button by text using the `buttonText` method:

```
var button = element(by.buttonText('Load Users'));
```

4. Now, click on the button to load the users:

```
button.click();
```

5. Find the element inside the `ng-repeat` directive using `by.repeater`:

```
var firstUsername = element(by.repeater('user in users')
                    .row(0).column('{{user.name}}'));
```

6. Next, add an expectation that the first element that displays the username is defined:

```
expect(firstUsername).toBeDefined();
```

7. Finally, add an expectation that the button is not displayed:

```
expect(button.isDisplayed()).toBeFalsy();
```

How it works...

In step 3, we use the `buttonText` locator (`http://angular.github.io/protractor/#/api?view=ProtractorBy.prototype.buttonText`) to find the filter button. In step 4, we click the button (`http://angular.github.io/protractor/#/api?view=webdriver.WebElement.prototype.click`), and this calls a handler to make the service request for users. We should expect at this point that we have a collection of users and our repeater should display at least one item.

In step 5, we use the repeater locator (`http://angular.github.io/protractor/#/api?view=ProtractorBy.prototype.repeater`) to find elements inside of an `ng-repeat` directive. The repeater locator API enables us to retrieve a specific row (`https://github.com/angular/protractor/blob/master/lib/locators.js#L293`) and column (`https://github.com/angular/protractor/blob/master/lib/locators.js#L318`) that expects a binding. We provide our `user.name` binding and then run an expectation that the element is defined.

Finally, in step 7, we test whether the element is currently displayed using the `isDisplayed` method (`http://angular.github.io/protractor/#/api?view=webdriver.WebElement.prototype.isDisplayed`).

See also

▶ The *Getting started with testing a service* recipe in this chapter

▶ The *Installing Protractor* recipe in *Chapter 1, Setup and Configuration*

9
A Brief Look at Testing Animations

In this chapter, you will learn the following recipes:

- ▸ Synchronous testing of animations
- ▸ Testing animations with ngAnimateMock
- ▸ Asynchronous testing of animations

Introduction

JavaScript, CSS3 transitions, and key frame animations offer a wealth of creative visual effects, for example when transitioning between two states. AngularJS offers hooks into these using the **ngAnimate** module. There are a range of directives that support animations, out of the box, and a full list can be found at `https://docs.angularjs.org/api/ngAnimate`. If you're looking for animation detection support while performing DOM operations in custom directives, then look no further than the `$animation` service (`https://docs.angularjs.org/api/ngAnimate/service/$animate`).

For information on animations, I highly recommend that you read this great article at `http://www.yearofmoo.com/2013/08/remastered-animation-in-angularjs-1-2.html#testing-animations`. This chapter will briefly introduce you to unit testing JavaScript animations, first using a synchronous approach and then asynchronously. The AngularJS team provides the animation mock module to help test animations (`https://github.com/angular/angular.js/blob/v1.2.26/src/ngMock/angular-mocks.js#L759`), which I will also demonstrate how to use in this chapter.

Synchronous testing of animations

This recipe will show you how to test a JavaScript animation in a synchronous approach by creating a mock replacement for the event handlers using the `$animateProvider` service.

Getting ready

For this example, you'll need a JavaScript animation that runs with show/hide options. I use jQuery (`http://jquery.com`) for the animations and transitions based on the opacity. The following are the steps to create the recipe test example :

1. Register a JavaScript animation via the `myModule.animation()` function. Also, create an object containing event callback animation functions that are triggered based on the ng-show animation event callbacks (`https://docs.angularjs.org/api/ng/directive/ngShow#animations`).

2. Secondly, add a class name to each of the callback's logic to check whether the `className` provided is `ng-hide`. Within the `beforeAddClass` callback, animate the element to opacity of value `0` and vice versa in the `removeClass` callback. Ensure that the `done` callback is made regardless of `className` in each function:

```
.animation('.js-fade', function() {
  return {
    beforeAddClass: function(element, className, done) {
      if (className === 'ng-hide') {
        element.animate({
          opacity: 0
        }, 1000, done);
      }
      else {
        done();
      }
    },
    removeClass: function(element, className, done) {
      if (className === 'ng-hide') {
        element.animate({
          opacity: 1
        }, 500, done);
      }
      else {
        done();
      }
    }
  };
})
```

3. Ensure that you've loaded AngularJS mocks (`https://code.angularjs.` `org/1.2.28/angular-mocks.js`) and AngularJS animate (`https://code.` `angularjs.org/1.2.28/angular-animate.js`) in your `SpecRunner.html` file.

4. Ensure that you've loaded your module, for example:

```
beforeEach(module('chapter9'));
```

How to do it...

Follow these steps to test JavaScript animations synchronously:

1. Create the following variables for the animation we're testing:
```
var scope;
var element;
var $rootElement;
var animatedShow = false;
var animatedHide = false;
```

2. Next, write a `beforeEach` function to inject the `$injector` service and retrieve our dependencies assigning them to the variables created in step 1:
```
beforeEach(inject(function($injector, $compile) {
  scope = $injector.get('$rootScope').$new();
  $rootElement = $injector.get('$rootElement');
}));
```

3. Within the `beforeEach` function in step 2, create a new AngularJS element using a string of HTML that adds a class named after our example JavaScript animation plus the ng-show directive based on a hint value:
```
element = angular.element('<div class="js-fade" ng-
show="hint"></div>');
```

4. Still within the `beforeEach` function in step 2, run the steps to compile and digest the element providing the scope object from step 2. Append the element returned to the `$rootElement` service (`https://docs.angularjs.org/api/ng/` `service/$rootElement`):
```
$compile(element)(scope);
scope.$digest();
$rootElement.append(element);
```

5. Next, within a `beforeEach` function use the `module` function to initialize an anonymous function:
```
beforeEach(module(function($animateProvider) {}));
```

6. Within the function, use the `$animateProvider` service to register our animation event handlers directly inside the module. Within each update, the corresponding Boolean values from step 1 need to be updated accordingly. We must also trigger the `done` callback:

```
$animateProvider.register('.js-fade', function() {
  return {
    beforeAddClass: function(element, className, done) {
      animatedHide = true;
      done();
    },
    removeClass: function(element, className, done) {
      animatedShow = true;
      done();
    }
  };
});
```

7. Next, create a test to ensure that the animation callback showing the element was called:

```
it('should animate to show', function() {});
```

8. Within the test, set the hint value on the scope to `true`:

```
Scope.hint = true;
```

9. Next, within the test, process all the watchers:

```
scope.$digest();
```

10. Finally, within the test created in step 7, add an expectation that the `animatedShow` Boolean value has been updated to `true`:

```
expect(animatedShow).toBeTruthy();
```

How it works...

We need an element to actually test our animation and additionally enable us to use the ng-show directive. This element is created in step 3 and adds the element CSS class attribute value to match the animation. If the `$animate` service discovers a match, then the callback function will be executed.

In step 6, we register mock JavaScript animation event handlers using the `$animateProvider` service. This is a key step to enable us to test our animation. AngularJS operates on the principle that whichever service is last registered with the `$injector` service will be the one provided when injected. So by registering an animation with the same name as the original from the application, we essentially ensure that our mock animation will be used. In step 6, we define the callback hooks mimicking our actual animation and update a Boolean value to test against.

In this recipe, we test whether the animation to display the element is functioning so we need to ensure that our `scope.hint` value is `true`; this we do in step 8. In step 10, we expect the ng-show directive to respond to the `scope.hint` value being `true` and display the element triggering the animation callback hooks and update our `animatedShow` value to `true`.

There's more...

To test whether the animation runs to hide the element, we can build on the preceding code and simply go through the motions to show and hide the element. Write a test as follows:

1. First, create a test that the animation callback for hiding the element was called:

   ```
   it('should animate to hide', function() {});
   ```

2. Next, within the test, set the hint value on the scope to `true` to show the animation, then `false`, and ensure that you digest the watchers in between each scope update:

   ```
   Scope.hint = true;
   Scope.$digest();
   Scope.hint = false;
   Scope.$digest();
   ```

3. Finally, add an expectation that the `animatedHide` Boolean value is updated to `true`:

   ```
   expect(animatedHide).toBeTruthy();
   ```

See also

▸ The *Asynchronous testing of animations* recipe in this chapter

▸ The *Testing animations with ngAnimateMock* recipe in this chapter

Testing animations with ngAnimateMock

The `ngAnimateMock` module replaces the `$animate` method with mock functions that are pushed into an animate queue. Each function has:

▸ Associated events, for example, `enter`

▸ Arguments, for example, class name

▸ An element

As opposed to the asynchronous approach, we cannot test the actual animation using the `ngAnimateMock` directive. Testing animations is a process of working through what animation logic has been added to the queue and whether it matches up to our expectations. In this recipe, we will test the enter event callback animation function, which appends the element to `parentElement` within the document and then runs the `enter` animation.

Getting ready

I use jQuery (`http://jquery.com`) for the animations and transitions based on the opacity. Here is the example code I use for testing this recipe that registers a JavaScript animation via the `myModule.animation()` function. I simply define an enter event callback animation function that animates the element to an opacity of 1:

```
.animation('.js-enter', function() {
  return {
    enter: function(element, className, done) {
      element.animate({
        opacity: 1
      }, done);
    }
  };
})
```

Ensure that you've loaded the AngularJS mocks file (`https://code.angularjs.org/1.2.28/angular-mocks.js`) and AngularJS animate (`https://code.angularjs.org/1.2.28/angular-animate.js`) in your `SpecRunner.html` file.

Also ensure that you've loaded your module including the AngularJS `ngAnimate` module, for example:

```
beforeEach(module('chapter9, ngAnimate'));
```

How to do it...

Follow these steps to test an animation using the `ngAnimateMock` directive:

1. Create the following variables for the animation we're testing:

    ```
    var scope;
    var element;
    var $rootElement;
    var $animate;
    ```

2. Next, write a `beforeEach` function to inject the `$injector` service and retrieve our dependencies assigning them to the variables created in step 1:

```
beforeEach(inject(function($injector, $compile) {
  scope = $injector.get('$rootScope').$new();
  $animate = $injector.get('$animate');
  $rootElement = $injector.get('$rootElement');
}));
```

3. Next, within the `beforeEach` function in step 2, create a new AngularJS element using a string of HTML that adds a class named after our example JavaScript animation:

```
element = angular.element('<div class="js-enter"></div>');
```

4. Create a test to check whether the element is appended to the parent element and create a variable for a queued object to be used in the expectation:

```
it('should append the element to parent element',
function() {
  var queuedObject;
});
```

5. Within the test, call the enter method providing the element created in step 3 and the `$rootElement` service from step 4:

```
$animate.enter(element, $rootElement);
```

6. Still within the test, remove the first element from the `$animate` queue assigning the value to the `queuedObject` variable from step 4:

```
queuedObject = $animate.queue.shift();
```

7. Finally, within the test created in step 4, run an expectation that the animated queue object HTML element is appended to the `$rootElement` service:

```
expect(queuedObject.element[0]).toEqual($rootElement.children()
[0]);
```

How it works...

In step 5, when we call the `enter` method providing the element and `$rootElement` as the only arguments that'll push an object into the queue. In step 6, we use the `shift()` method (https://developer.mozilla.org/en-US/docs/Web/JavaScript/Reference/Global_Objects/Array/shift) to remove the first element in the queue and store the returned object. We can then retrieve the element of that object and compare it against the actual object that the `$animate` service adds to the parent object (`$rootElement`).

See also

▶ The *Synchronous testing of animations* recipe in this chapter

▶ The *Asynchronous testing of animations* recipe in this chapter

Asynchronous testing of animations

This recipe will show you how to test a JavaScript animation in an asynchronous fashion. There are (as with most things) pros and cons to this approach. You will see in this recipe with asynchronous testing that we can verify whether the relevant CSS properties were updated. However, to do this, we need to wait for the transition time to complete, which increases the time it takes for our tests to complete.

Getting ready

Please refer to the *Getting ready* section in the *Synchronous testing of animations* recipe in this chapter. Ensure that you've loaded AngularJS animate (`https://code.angularjs.org/1.2.28/angular-animate.js`) in your `SpecRunner.html` file.

Also, ensure that you've loaded your module, for example:

```
beforeEach(module('chapter9'));
```

How to do it...

Follow these steps to test JavaScript animations asynchronously:

1. Create the following variables for the animation we're testing:

```
var scope;
var element;
var $rootElement;
```

2. Next, write a `beforeEach` function to inject the `$injector` service and retrieve our dependencies assigning them to the variables created in step 1:

```
beforeEach(inject(function($injector, $compile) {
  scope = $injector.get('$rootScope').$new();
  $rootElement = $injector.get('$rootElement');
}));
```

3. Next, within the `beforeEach` function in step 2, create a new AngularJS element using a string of HTML that adds a class named after our example JavaScript animation plus the ng-show directive based on a hint value:

```
element = angular.element('<div class="js-fade" ng-show="hint"></
div>');
```

4. Still within the `beforeEach` function in step 2, run the steps to compile and digest the element providing the scope object from step 2. Append the element returned to the `$rootElement` service (`https://docs.angularjs.org/api/ng/service/$rootElement`):

```
$compile(element)(scope);
scope.$digest();
$rootElement.append(element);
```

5. Create a test to ensure that the element animates to an opacity of `0` value:

```
it('should animate to an opacity of 0', function(done) {});
```

6. Next, within the test, set the hint value on the scope to `true` to show the animation, then `false`, and ensure that you digest the watchers in between each scope update:

```
Scope.hint = true;
Scope.$digest();
Scope.hint = false;
Scope.$digest();
```

7. Finally, within a `setTimeout` function, add an expectation that the opacity of the element is now less than value `1` and call the done callback:

```
setTimeout(function() {
  expect(element.css('opacity') < 1).toBeTruthy();
  done();
}, 1000);
```

How it works...

Step 3 starts with defining our Angular element with the CSS class attribute matching the animation and the ng-show directive. We use Jasmine's asynchronous support (`http://jasmine.github.io/2.0/introduction.html#section-Asynchronous_Support`) to enable us to decide when the spec will be run. Providing the `done` argument to our test function, as seen in step 5, informs Jasmine that we are running an asynchronous test. Step 6 sets the `scope.hint` value to `true`, and this will display the element. Then we set the value to `false` that will hide the element and trigger the animation.

Our expectation has to be executed after the given time for the element transition to take place; therefore the logic is hooked into a `setTimeout` function (`https://developer.mozilla.org/en-US/docs/Web/API/WindowTimers.setTimeout`). Also, within the `setTimeout` function we ensured that the `done()` callback is called so that Jasmine runs the test.

See also

- ▸ The *Synchronous testing of animations* recipe in this chapter
- ▸ The *Testing animations with ngAnimateMock* recipe in this chapter

Index

Symbols

$httpBackend service
  used, for testing HTTP GET
      requests 122, 123
  used, for testing HTTP POST
      requests 124-126

A

angular animate
  reference link 145
angular-debaser library
  reference link 34
AngularJS
  about 1, 45
  URL, for tutorial 4
AngularJS code
  debugging 37-39
AngularJS elements
  reference link 103
angular.js file
  URL, for downloading 33
angular.mock.module function 32, 33
angular-mocks.js file
  URL, for downloading 33
angular-mocks.js library 7
animations
  asynchronous testing 150, 151
  references 143
  synchronous testing 144-147
  testing, with ngAnimateMock
      module 147-149
API methods, Protractor
  URL 10
asynchronous testing,
     of animations 150, 151

B

basic AngularJS application
  creating 2-4
basic html content
  accessing 84
Batarang
  about 39
  URL 39
Behavior-Driven Development (BDD) 31
Brunch
  URL 25

C

Chrome
  URL 9
Chrome DevTools, Twitter feed
  reference link 39
class changes, based on windows
      properties 91-93
clean slate 32
configuration file docs, Testem
  URL 20
configuration, of ngRoute
  reference link 47
configuration options, Karma
  autoWatch 17
  Browsers 17
  files 17
  frameworks 17
configuration options, Testem
  framework 20
  launch_in_dev 20
  src_files 20

Thank you for buying
AngularJS Testing Cookbook

About Packt Publishing

Packt, pronounced 'packed', published its first book, *Mastering phpMyAdmin for Effective MySQL Management*, in April 2004, and subsequently continued to specialize in publishing highly focused books on specific technologies and solutions.

Our books and publications share the experiences of your fellow IT professionals in adapting and customizing today's systems, applications, and frameworks. Our solution-based books give you the knowledge and power to customize the software and technologies you're using to get the job done. Packt books are more specific and less general than the IT books you have seen in the past. Our unique business model allows us to bring you more focused information, giving you more of what you need to know, and less of what you don't.

Packt is a modern yet unique publishing company that focuses on producing quality, cutting-edge books for communities of developers, administrators, and newbies alike. For more information, please visit our website at www.packtpub.com.

About Packt Open Source

In 2010, Packt launched two new brands, Packt Open Source and Packt Enterprise, in order to continue its focus on specialization. This book is part of the Packt open source brand, home to books published on software built around open source licenses, and offering information to anybody from advanced developers to budding web designers. The Open Source brand also runs Packt's open source Royalty Scheme, by which Packt gives a royalty to each open source project about whose software a book is sold.

Writing for Packt

We welcome all inquiries from people who are interested in authoring. Book proposals should be sent to author@packtpub.com. If your book idea is still at an early stage and you would like to discuss it first before writing a formal book proposal, then please contact us; one of our commissioning editors will get in touch with you.

We're not just looking for published authors; if you have strong technical skills but no writing experience, our experienced editors can help you develop a writing career, or simply get some additional reward for your expertise.

[PACKT] open source
community experience distilled
PUBLISHING

Mastering AngularJS Directives

Develop, maintain, and test production-ready directives for any AngularJS-based application

Josh Kurz   [PACKT] open source

Mastering AngularJS Directives

ISBN: 978-1-78398-158-8   Paperback: 210 pages

Develop, maintain, and test production-ready directives for any AngularJS-based application

1. Explore the options available for creating directives, by reviewing detailed explanations and real-world examples.

2. Dissect the life cycle of a directive and understand why they are the base of the AngularJS framework.

3. Discover how to create structured, maintainable, and testable directives through a step-by-step, hands-on approach to AngularJS.

Mastering Web Application Development with AngularJS

Build single-page web applications using the power of AngularJS

Pawel Kozlowski
Peter Bacon Darwin   [PACKT] open source

Mastering Web Application Development with AngularJS

ISBN: 978-1-78216-182-0   Paperback: 372 pages

Build single-page web applications using the power of AngularJS

1. Make the most out of AngularJS by understanding the AngularJS philosophy and applying it to real-life development tasks.

2. Effectively structure, write, test, and finally deploy your application.

3. Add security and optimization features to your AngularJS applications.

4. Harness the full power of AngularJS by creating your own directives.

Please check **www.PacktPub.com** for information on our titles

AngularJS UI Development

ISBN: 978-1-78328-847-2   Paperback: 258 pages

Design, build, and test production-ready applications in AngularJS

1. Design and customize applications with mobile users in mind using open source CSS3 frameworks.

2. Use polished UI components written from scratch solely in AngularJS to build real-world applications with a comprehensive, step-by-step guide.

3. Learn using a proven workflow from setting up the environment to testing in order to be productive in writing ambitious applications.

Deploying AngularJS [Video]

ISBN: 978-1-78355-447-8   Duration: 01:37 hours

Application development and deployment made easy with AngularJS and Heroku

1. Create an easy-to-understand and flexible build system for your application using GulpJS.

2. Deploy to Heroku and add monitoring tools for error tracking.

3. Beginner-friendly introduction to writing tests and utilizing best practices.

Please check **www.PacktPub.com** for information on our titles

Lightning Source UK Ltd.
Milton Keynes UK
UKOW07f0203110715

254966UK00003B/44/P